The Revelation:
Discussion and Study Guide

By

Joseph McRae Mellichamp

Thousand Fields Publishing
www.1000fieldspub.com

To Followers of Jesus Who Want to Know His Plans for the Future

The Revelation:
Discussion and Study Guide

THE REVELATION: DISCUSSION AND STUDY GUIDE
Foreword

Some forty years ago, I don't remember the exact date, but a few years after I became a committed follower of Jesus, I heard about a book that was all the rage in Christian circles. The book: *The Late Great Planet Earth*, by Hal Lindsey, a "penetrating look at incredible prophecies involving this generation" [Grand Rapids, MI: Zondervan Publishing House]. The book had an original copyright date of 1970; the copy I have on my bookshelf is the "One Millionth Copy Edition," apparently printed in 1972.

I read the book along with many of my Christian friends and actually led a couples Bible study for about a dozen friends using the book as our primary reference. For those of you who were around in those days, they were pretty scary times. We were in the midst of the Cold War with the former Soviet Union—hostilities which would last until the Iron Curtin fell in 1989 and which look to be heating up again. We had survived the energy crisis of the early 1970s and were experiencing double digit inflation and uncertain economic times. And Lindsey's book didn't offer much hope.

In Chapter 14 titled "Polishing the Crystal Ball," he writes, "Now I am about to walk into the lion's den. ... [I]n this chapter I will make a number of forecasts about the future which are based on a careful study of the prophetic truth and the writings of many scholars on the subject." And his prophecies which cover the religious scene, the political scene, and the sociological scene are very grim indeed. In fact, according to Lindsey then, our only hope for America was "a widespread spiritual awakening."

I've spent my adult life as a scholar having conducted research and taught as a university professor and writer for almost fifty years. But my area of expertise was management science, which is the application of mathematical and computer technology to problems of business, industry, and government. Back in Hal

Lindsey's heyday, I was a Bible neophyte. I was impressed with Lindsey's attempt to understand the times in the light of Biblical prophecy, but I thought he made some leaps beyond the data in some of his assertions.

I retired from the world of academia twenty years ago and have been blessed to spend much of my time since then studying the Bible and leading studies for laypersons here in the Atlanta suburbs where we moved upon retirement. In 2008, I decided to bite the proverbial bullet, roll up my sleeves, and tackle teaching through the book of The Revelation. One of the first references I acquired, which aided my inquiries tremendously, was *Revelation Four Views: A Parallel Commentary* by Steve Gregg [Nashville, TN: Thomas Nelson Publishers, 1997].

The thing I really appreciated about Gregg's approach is that he lays out the four different approaches to understanding this mysterious book [we will cover these shortly], giving an unbiased presentation of each. He hopes that when the reader finishes reading the book, or working through it, he or she won't know which of the four approaches Gregg personally accepts. And I think for Gregg's purposes—to compare the four approaches—it makes sense to proceed in a neutral way. I also believe that there are sound reasons, which I will enumerate, for favoring one of the approaches [the Spiritual] over the others. Thus in these study notes, I have followed that particular interpretation approach while trying in the process to point out how that approach differs from the other approaches.

In the notes which follow I present an introduction to the book which covers the *who, what, when, where, why,* and *so what* information that is necessary to understand a particular book. Then I discuss the four interpretation approaches giving arguments for and against each one. This is followed by a discussion of how the book is organized and some principles we will follow in interpreting the book. Next I give an overview of the book making use of a book chart which shows the organization of the book in graphic form along with a list of symbols and their meanings that one will encounter in the text. Finally, I give detailed outlines for each of the book's twenty-two chapters along with application questions. In these questions I have embedded thorough discussion of what the elements in the text symbolize, primarily using the spiritual interpretation approach. *Comparative Notes* are interspersed throughout the text to show how the major sections of the book are viewed by each of the four interpretation approaches.

I recently finished leading a study of C.S. Lewis' great classic **Mere Christianity** to a group of friends in our neighborhood. At our last meeting, I attached a gold star to the Study Guide of each of the neighbors who had completed the study, because the book is, for sure, a challenging read. If **Mere Christianity** is a tough read, **The Revelation** is Mount Everest! There are things in the book that we simply don't have a clue as to what they mean and this side of Heaven, we probably can't know what they mean. So our attitude as we begin is to "bite the bullet, roll up our sleeves, and tackle" this great book, realizing that we won't get everything right, we'll have to admit we are stumped from time to time and that is OK, because we know we will be blessed for making the attempt (Revelation 1:3).

And if you have a good teacher, he or she might just give you a gold star when you finish your study! Enjoy the journey.

THE REVELATION
Introduction

Who?

It is generally believed that John the beloved Apostle, the Galilean fisherman, and son of Zebedee, was the recipient of The Revelation from Jesus and recorded it for the benefit of all believers. Here are the different arguments you will encounter on the authorship of The Revelation.

Steve Gregg in *Revelation Four Views: A Parallel Commentary* [Nashville, TN: Thomas Nelson Publishers, 1997] offers the following on authorship.

Arguments for John's Authorship:
- The author identifies himself as "John." Revelation 1:1,4; 22:8
- The early church fathers attributed the book to John the Apostle.
  - Justin Martyr (165).
  - Irenaeus (180).
  - Clement of Alexandria (215).
  - Tertullian (220).

Arguments Against John's Authorship:
- Some later church fathers attributed the book to another John.
  - Dionysius of Alexandria (250 c).
  - Eusebius (325).
- Contrasts in style among John (Gospel), John (letters) and The Revelation.
  - Gospel and letters are "good" Greek style.
  - The Revelation is "stumbling" with "many grammatical laxities."

Responses to Arguments Against:
- John may have used a secretary for the Gospel and letters, and would not have had access to one for The Revelation.

1

- No other person in New Testament church could have identified himself simply as "John" and expected to be known.
- Many concepts and expressions are common to the Gospel, the letters and The Revelation.
  - Logos (Word). John 1:1 and Revelation 19:13
  - The Lamb. John 1:29, 36 and Revelation 5:6
  - Water of Life. John 7:37 and Revelation 22:17

William Hendriksen in *More Than Conquerors: An Interpretation of the Book of Revelation* [Grand Rapids, MI: Baker Book House, 1940] offers the following on authorship.

Arguments against John's Authorship:
- The author of the Gospel and the letters never identifies himself.
- There is a contrast in style and general tone between the Gospel and Revelation.
  - John: God's love; Revelation: God's justice.
  - John: heart condition; Revelation: world events.
  - John: beautiful, idiomatic Greek; Revelation: rugged Hebrew, barbarous Greek.
- There is a contrast in doctrine between the Gospel and Revelation.
  - John: broad-minded and universalistic.
  - Revelation: narrow-minded and particularistic.

Arguments for John's Authorship:
- The fact that the author of The Revelation identifies himself and the author of the Gospel and the letters does not, proves nothing.
- The style differences may be explained by the fact that John is writing different genres: history, letters, and apocalypse.
- Hendriksen argues that there are no doctrinal differences whatsoever!
- The early church fathers attributed the book to John the Apostle.
  - Justin Martyr (165).

2

- Irenaeus (180).
- Muratorian Canon (170).
- Clement of Alexandria (215).
- Tertullian (220).
- Origin of Alexandria (223).
- John was a resident of Ephesus to which the first of the seven letters to the churches in Revelation was addressed.

What?

Gregg offers a number of explanations for what The Revelation actually is:
- Apocalyptic, Greek revelation. Written to reveal certain mysteries about heaven and earth, humankind and God, angels and demons, the world today and the world to come.
- One of the main themes of the book is that great suffering lies ahead; martyrdom is also a recurring theme.
- The book uses vivid images and symbols in depicting the conflict between good and evil.
- The book employs numbers to convey concepts rather than merely counting units.

Hendriksen gives a slightly different take on his view of what this book represents:
- The theme of the book is the victory of Christ and His Church over the dragon (Satan) and his helpers.
- Jesus is depicted as the Victor over death, Hades, the dragon, the beast, the false prophet, and the men who worship the beast. He is victorious and, as a result, so are we even though we appear to be hopelessly defeated (Revelation 17:14).

When?

Most scholars believe the book was written in the 90s AD, probably 95 AD. Here are Gregg's arguments:

- Ten Roman emperors persecuted Christians; only two within John's lifetime: Nero (54-68) and Domitian (81-96).
- Nero's persecution never extended far beyond Rome itself; Domitian's extended throughout the empire.
- The churches were all founded too near to Nero's persecution for the conditions prevailing in four of them to have materialized for an early date.
  - Ephesus (founded 52) had left its first love.
  - Laodicea (founded 52) was lukewarm.
  - Pergamum (founded 52) had embraced false doctrine.
  - Thyatira (founded 50s) had conformed to the culture.
- A passage from Irenaeus seems to suggest that Revelation was written during the reign of Domitian, but the meaning of the text is unclear.

Hendriksen provides an additional three clues that help us date the book in the 90s:
- One cannot find a single cogent argument in favor of the earlier date (69) that some scholars associate with Revelation.
- When the book was written, John had been banished, a very common form of punishment during Domitian's reign.
- By the time of Domitian's reign, the Roman Empire had become the great antagonist of the Christian Church.

Where?

- From where was The Revelation written? Patmos, Revelation 1:9.
- To whom was The Revelation written?
  - The book was intended for believers in John's day and age. It owed its origin to contemporary conditions. It is God's answer to persecuted Christians in Asia Minor.
  - The book was intended by God not only for those who first read it, but for all believers throughout the Church Age.

Why?

Hendriksen and Gregg combine to give us three reasons for the book:
- Revelation is God's answer to the prayers and tears of severely persecuted Christians scattered in the cities of Asia Minor and for believers throughout the Church Age.
- Revelation itself claims to be inspired by God to predict the future—thus it claims to be prophetic writing.
- Revelation was written during a time of intense persecution of Christians—it has been called "a tract for hard times."

So What?

1. Revelation is a really difficult book to understand, and we can't be entirely certain that we have understood it correctly. So why don't we just punt it and move on to something easier?
2. Why is it important to know who wrote the different books of the Bible? Does it make any difference whether The Revelation was written by John the Apostle or someone else? Do you feel reasonably assured, given the material we have discussed, that John the Apostle was our man?
3. Persecution of Christians is a fact of history. Have you ever been persecuted because of your faith in Christ, or is persecution something that only happens in Middle Eastern countries? Do you need a "tract for hard times?"
4. I have argued many times that it really matters when the different books of the Bible were written. We think The Revelation was written around 95AD. Why does this matter?
5. What would you say to a friend whom you invited to our study of The Revelation who replied, "Oh I don't think you can make any sense at all out of all that symbolism—it is a waste of time?"

THE REVELATION
Approaches to Interpretation

Approaches

Bible scholars recognize four different approaches to interpreting the Book of the Revelation: the historicist, Preterist, futurist and spiritual approaches. See Revelation Interpretation Approaches Timelines on page 14 and 144.

Historicist Approach

Those who hold to the historicist view believe that God revealed the entire church age in advance through the symbolic visions of the Apocalypse. The historicist believes we are able to align specific historical events with certain details in Revelation; for example, the breaking of the seven seals in Chapters 6 and 7 is often said to correspond to the barbarian invasions that sacked the Western Roman Empire.

- Very few Bible scholars today hold to this position, but many notables of the past including John Wycliffe, John Knox, William Tyndale, Martin Luther, John Calvin, Sir Isaac Newton, John Wesley, Jonathan Edwards, George Whitefield, C.H. Spurgeon, and Matthew Henry embraced the historicist approach.
- One non-negotiable feature of classical historicist exposition is the assertion that the papacy (Catholic Church) is "Antichrist." And since the Reformers were the principal adherents of this approach, some scholars have suggested they adopted what turns out to be a weak theological position to discredit their main protagonist.

Arguments for:
- Gregg writes, "When one examines the verse-by-verse expositions of the historicists, I think one will have to say that the scheme makes more than a few occasional hits."

6

- When the view predominated, it was said, "A missionary could go to heathen lands armed with a copy of *The Rise and Fall of the Roman Empire* and Barnes' *Notes on Revelation* and prove the inspiration of Scripture beyond question."

Arguments Against:
- One of the weaknesses of the approach is the inability of its advocates to agree on the specific fulfillment of the prophecies.
- Another criticism of the approach is that it is too flexible in the service of its advocates, allowing them to identify their own times as the culmination of history.
- It is also criticized as being too parochial, failing to take the development of the church throughout the world into consideration.
- Moreover, the approach concerns itself mainly with the period of the Middle Ages and the Reformation and has relatively little to say of events after 1500.

Reference: Barnes, Albert, "Revelation" in *Notes on the New Testament*, Grand Rapids, MI: Baker Book House, 1884-85.

Preterist Approach

Among those identifying themselves as Preterists, there are two types:

1. Contemporary-historical. Proponents believe that contemporary features of John's own day can be identified in the symbolic language he uses. But they don't generally insist upon any actual fulfillment in the ensuing events of the things prophesied in the Apocalypse.
   - They almost all believe in a date of writing in Domitian's reign (95-96 AD) and believe that John's desire for a quick vindication in the coming of the kingdom was expressed in his prophecy, but failed to be fulfilled.

- Some of these scholars have no respect whatever for the Apocalypse as an inspired writing, and have been called by some "the Left-Wing" of Preterism.
2. Classical. Those who hold to the classical Preterism of past centuries take a high view of the inspiration of Scripture and date the Book of Revelation prior to 70 AD. They believe that many details in Revelation were fulfilled in the fall of Jerusalem (70 AD); other details they suggest are predictions of the fall of the Roman Empire and the second coming of Christ.

[The arguments for and against which follow are for classical Preterism, not contemporary-historical Preterism.]

Arguments for:
- Some scholars assert that since Matthew (24), Mark (13), and Luke (17,21) all relate Jesus' Olivet Discourse, often called the little apocalypse, Revelation is John's expanded version of Jesus' prophecy concerning Jerusalem.
- Some early church fathers (Eusebius 325 AD) recognized in the Olivet Discourse a description of Jerusalem's destruction by the Romans. However Eusebius did not himself extend the application to Revelation.

Arguments against:
- The principal criticism of the Preterist approach is its heavy dependence on the pre-AD 70 date of writing, which is defensible, but disputed.
- Another criticism of Preterism relates to its roots. Some have suggested that it originated as a Roman Catholic response to the Reformer's historicism.

Reference: Clark, David S., *The Message from Patmos: A Postmillennial Commentary on the Book of Revelation*, Grand Rapids, MI: Baker Book House, 1989.

Futurist Approach

According to this view, Revelation divides into three sections, given in 1:19, where John is told to write "the things which you have seen, and the things which are, and the things which shall be after these things.

- Accordingly, we have:
    - Chapter 1: The things John had seen.
    - Chapter 2-3: The things which are.
    - Chapter 4-22: Things future to John and to us today.
- Most of the material (Chapters 6-19) is held to describe a seven-year Tribulation period, followed by the return of Christ (19), a thousand-year reign of Christ on earth (20), and the new creation (21-22).

Arguments for:
- Belief in the futurist approach frees the reader to take a more literal view of the visions (since everything is yet to happen), reducing the difficulty of interpreting symbols.
- And it is probably this desire to interpret the vision literally, more than anything else, which accounts for the popularity of the approach. Proponents of the approach include: Hal Lindsey, Charles Ryrie, John Walvoord, and C.I. Schofield.

Arguments against:
- Some scholars insist that futurism, like historicism, renders the Book of Revelation about 90 percent irrelevant to the original readers since they lived at least 2,000 years prior to its fulfillment.
- Others object to its origins as a protest approach fabricated by a Jesuit priest in 1585 to counter the historicism of the Reformers and their insistence that the "beast" was the papacy.
- One additional problem with the futurist approach is that it cannot be tested from history as the historicist and Preterist approaches can. Whether this is an asset or liability to futurism is not a matter of universal agreement.

9

Reference: Lindsey, Hal, *There's a New World Coming: A Prophetic Odyssey*, Eugene, OR: Harvest House, 1973.

Spiritual Approach

According to the spiritual view, the great themes of the triumph of good over evil, of Christ over Satan, of the vindication of the martyrs and the sovereignty of God are played out throughout Revelation without necessary reference to specific historical events. Spiritual lessons and principles, which may find recurrent expressions in history, are depicted symbolically in the vision.

- Thus, the battles in Revelation may be seen as referring to spiritual warfare, to the persecution of Christians, or to natural warfare in general throughout history.
- To call this the spiritual approach is not to call into question the spirituality of the other approaches but to distinguish it from the more historical focus of the others.

Arguments for:
- The most significant advantage of the spiritual approach is that it avoids the problem of harmonizing specific passages with specific fulfillments.
- It is relatively easy to combine the approach with the historicist or Preterist approach, because the symbols can be associated with historical events.

Arguments against:
- Probably the strongest argument against this approach is that the book itself claims that the events it is predicting will shortly come to pass.
- The spiritual approach is sometimes associated with theological liberalism; but it is entirely consistent with a high view of inspiration of Scripture.

Reference: Hendriksen, William, *More Than Conquerors: An Interpretation of the Book of Revelation*, Grand Rapids, MI: Baker Book House, 1939.

Views of the Millennium

The greatest issue of controversy related to the book of Revelation, from earliest times to the present, is related to one's understanding of the meaning of the "thousand years" in Revelation 20. The term "Millennium" [Latin: *mille*=thousand, and *annus*=years] has generally been adopted to refer to this period. Only this one chapter in the entire Bible mentions the thousand-year reign of the saints with Christ; some characterize this as the most controversial chapter in the Bible.

Most agree that the chapter refers to the same period as that depicted in many Old Testament passages describing the golden age of the Messiah including, Psalms 72 and 110; Isaiah 2:1-4, 11:1-11; Ezekiel 34; and Daniel 2. There has never been universal agreement in the church regarding the meaning of these passages. Three Christian views on the Millennium are generally recognized:

Premillennialism

This is the view that the second coming of Christ will precede the millennial kingdom. Taking a mostly literal approach, advocates of this view expect a period of one thousand year's duration in which Christ will reign with His saints here on earth prior to the eternal new heaven and new earth. Dispensational premillennialism differs from historic premillennialism in its emphasis on the continued centrality of the nation of Israel in God's plan for the future and in anticipating a Rapture—the removal of Christians from earth to heaven before the beginning of the Tribulation.

Postmillennialism

This view holds that Christ returns after the millennial period, which will be established through the evangelistic mission of the church. This enterprise will be so successful that all or most people will become Christians, resulting in a thousand years of peace on earth before Christ's second coming.

Amillennialism

Some see the thousand years of Revelation as symbolic of an indefinitely long period of time corresponding to the entire span of time from the first coming of Christ to His second coming. Most aspects of chapter 20, like most aspects of the entire book are believed to be symbolic. The binding of Satan happened spiritually at the Cross, the reign of the saints is the present age, the loosing of Satan is a final period of deception coming at the end of the age, and the fire from heaven that devours the wicked is the second coming of Christ.

It should be underscored that the four approaches to interpreting Revelation are not linked inseparably to any particular millennial position, so that one's eschatological (millennial) position does not dictate which approach to interpretation must be employed.

- In general, those adopting a futurist view in interpretation would most likely identify with premillennialism and those subscribing to the Preterist view of interpretation are often, but not always, inclined toward postmillennialism.
- Those holding to amillennialism have included virtually every theologian from Augustine through the Reformation, with many adherents today.
- Amillennialists have held to each of the four approaches to interpretation, including Martin Luther (historicist), Jay Adams (Preterist), William Hendriksen (spiritual), and Abraham Kuyper (futurist).

Applications

1. You should have concluded by now that many intelligent people have studied this book of the Bible without coming to unanimous agreement about how to understand its message.

Do you find this disconcerting, or are you willing to look at the book from one of the four interpretation approaches to see what we can learn?

2. The chart shown on page 144 should convince even the most ardent devotee of one of the other approaches to understanding the Revelation that the spiritual approach is the view held by the church almost from the time John wrote the book. The other three approaches were primarily reactionary views and don't therefore warrant the same consideration as the Spiritual approach. What do you think?

3. I have always felt that God is an industrial engineer at heart— He is very efficient and doesn't waste words, experiences, or resources. To me it doesn't make sense that He would give us a book which would be of little benefit to any believer who lived from 70 AD to the present (and beyond); thus, I don't think the Futurist Approach merits more than passing consideration. Are you OK with my reasoning?

4. As we proceed through our study, we will examine the book from a predominantly spiritual approach, but we will try to see how this approach differs from the other three approaches, at least in macro respects. Are you OK with this approach?

5. Of the four approaches to interpretation, the historicist view is waning, the Preterist is a minority view, while many today hold to the futurist and the spiritual approaches. Can you explain why this is so?

6. One of the great criticisms of the world today toward Christians is that we are literalists. Is this a bad thing? Shouldn't we affirm and embrace the clear teaching of Scripture. Do you see that by taking a spiritualist approach to interpreting Revelation, we open ourselves up to being labeled anti-literalists?

7. This study is going to be a real challenge. We are going to have to roll up our sleeves and dig deep in order to understand what God has for us in this great book. Are you up for the challenge?

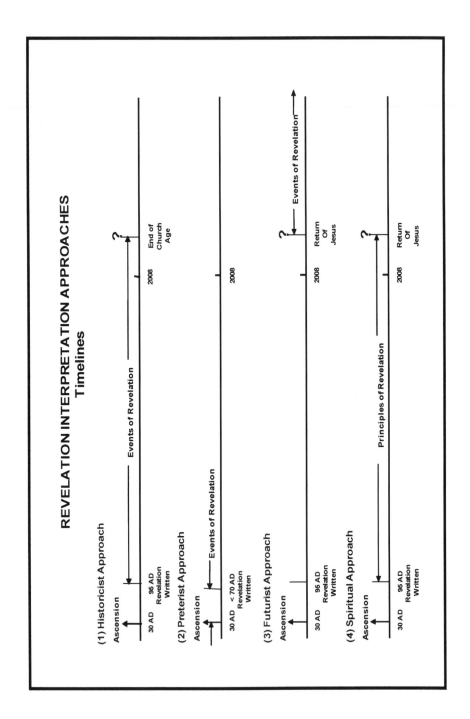

REVELATION INTERPRETATION APPROACHES
Timelines

(1) Historicist Approach

Ascension

30 AD   95 AD
         Revelation
         Written

Events of Revelation

2008   End of
        Church
        Age

?

(2) Preterist Approach

Ascension

Events of Revelation

30 AD   < 70 AD
        Revelation
        Written

2008

(3) Futurist Approach

Ascension

30 AD   95 AD
         Revelation
         Written

2008   Return
        Of
        Jesus

?

Events of Revelation

(4) Spiritual Approach

Ascension

30 AD   95 AD
         Revelation
         Written

Principles of Revelation

2008   Return
        Of
        Jesus

?

14

THE REVELATION
Organization and Analysis

For the remainder of our study, we will be following the spiritual approach to interpreting The Revelation; our primary reference will be the book itself and our secondary reference will be William Hendriksen, *More Than Conquerors: An Interpretation of the Book of Revelation,* Grand Rapids, MI: Baker Book House, 1940. In his book, Hendriksen gives nine principles (he calls them propositions) for interpreting [understanding] the book which we will consider here as we begin an overview and analysis of John's Apocalypse.

Principle 1. The Revelation consists of seven sections which are parallel and span the entire dispensation, from the first to the second coming of Christ.

Principle 2. The seven sections may be grouped into two major divisions which reveal a progress in depth or intensity of spiritual conflict. The first division (Chapters 1-11) reveals the Church, indwelt by Christ, persecuted by the world. The second division reveals the deeper spiritual background of this struggle—it is a conflict between Christ and the dragon in which Christ, and His Church, are victorious.

Given these two principles, we are now in a position to consider how the book is organized and we do so by presenting the following outline.

Outline

I. The Struggle on Earth. Chapters 1-11. [The Church persecuted by the world. The Church is avenged, protected and victorious.]
    A. Christ in the midst of the seven lampstands. Chapters 1-3
    B. The scroll with seven seals. Chapters 4-7
    C. The seven trumpets of judgment. Chapters 8-11

II. The Cosmic Struggle. Chapters 12-22. [Christ and the Church persecuted by the dragon (Satan) and his helpers. Christ and His Church are victorious.]
   A. The Woman and the Child persecuted. Chapters 12-14
   B. The seven bowls of wrath. Chapters 15-16
   C. The fall of the harlot and the beasts. Chapters 17-19
   D. Judgment upon the dragon; new heaven, earth; new Jerusalem. Chapters 20-22

In the first division, we see the struggle among men, that is, between believers and unbelievers. The world (unbelievers) attacks the Church (believers). In the second division we are shown that this struggle on earth has deeper significance.

The second division answers the following questions: (1) What is the underlying cause of the persecution of the church by the world? In other words, why do unbelievers hate believers so vehemently? What is behind this? and (2) What is going to happen to impenitent individuals who do not heed God's warning voice revealed in the trumpets of judgment?

Principle 3. The book is one—it is a unity. The principles of human conduct and divine moral government are progressively revealed; the lampstands give rise to the seals, the seals to the trumpets, and so on.

Several points reinforce this argument:
- Chapter 1 is closely connected to Chapters 2 and 3. One must understand how the three chapters hang together.
- The Church reveals the light of heaven to a world that lies in darkness. And the Church needs affliction in order that it may be cleansed.
- Wherever and whenever Christ enters upon the scene of history, the sword is bound to appear. His disciples become cross-bearers; peace is affected.

- What happens when Christ's warnings of judgment do not result in penitence and conversion? Will the Ruler of the universe overlook such hardness of heart?

Principle 4. The seven sections of Revelation are arranged in ascending, climactic order. There is progress in the order of prophecy with increasing intensity.

Several points reinforce this argument:
- Revelation, according to Hendriksen is at once simple and profound. It gives us the real philosophy of history. It shows us principles of human and satanic conduct and of divine moral government as they are revealing themselves.
- Throughout history, warnings of judgment always precede bowls (events) of wrath when the warnings are unheeded.
- The closer we get to the end of the book the more our attention is directed to the final judgment and that which lies behind it.
- In the first division, the final judgment is only introduced; in the second division, it is described in symbolic detail.

Principle 5. The fabric of the book consists of moving pictures. The details that pertain to the pictures should be interpreted in harmony with the book's central thought. We should ask two questions. First, what is the entire picture? Second, what is its predominant idea?

Several points reinforce this argument:
- Just as in interpreting parables, one must concentrate on the central truth of the story; in considering the Apocalypse, one must not let the details obscure the larger picture.
- What we are after is the total impression, the central idea of each of the individual pictures which are used to convey the larger truth.

Principle 6. The different symbols—seals, trumpets, bowls of wrath, etc.—refer not to specific events, particular happenings, or details of history, but to principles—of human conduct and divine

17

moral government—that are operating throughout the history of the world, especially through the church age.

- The symbols usually come in groups of seven—this is not likely to happen in the messy, unordered world of real life. We do have a saying, "Trouble comes in sets of three."
- We should constantly bear in mind that the purpose of God is to make men wise unto salvation. The book has an ethical and a spiritual purpose.

Principle 7. The Apocalypse is rooted in contemporaneous events and circumstances. Its symbols should be interpreted in the light of conditions which prevailed when the book was written [90s AD]

- The Apocalypse had as its immediate purpose the strengthening of the wavering hearts of the persecuted believers of the first century AD.
- The book is replete with references to contemporaneous events and circumstances. Thus, John's readers would have been interested in the struggle being waged in their own time.
- Of course, the book spans the entire church age and is intended for us as well as first century believers. But it was occasioned by suffering first century Christians.

Principle 8. The Apocalypse is rooted in the sacred Scriptures. It should be interpreted in harmony with the teachings of the entire Bible. See page 145.

- The Apocalypse must be understood not only in light of external events but of the entire religious heritage of believers at the time of writing.
- We must permit Scripture to interpret Scripture. This implies first giving credence to the immediate context in which a passage occurs.
- Once the context has been duly considered, parallel passages [there are hundreds] should be taken into account in this order: the Apocalypse, the New Testament, and then the Old Testament.

18

Principle 9. The Apocalypse is rooted in the mind and revelation of God. God in Christ is the real author, and this book contains the purpose of God concerning the history of the Church.

- God prepared and formed the soul of John the apostle so that he was able to receive and record this glorious prophecy.
- The God who inspired all of the sacred writings so that they are all God-breathed is also the Author of the Apocalypse.

Applications

1. The outline Hendriksen provides for us is pretty simple: two major divisions, three sections in one division, four in another. The first division is set on earth and describes earthly struggles of believers and unbelievers; the second division is set in the heavens and gives the reasons for the earthly conflict. Do you understand this? How can you remind yourself from time to time?

2. It can't be emphasized enough that the events described in these passages are parallel in the sense that they are taking place throughout the Church age—from Christ's first coming to His second coming. Do you understand how it is problematic to attempt to identify the events of the prophecy with specific events in history?

3. Hendriksen warns us against getting so caught up in the details of symbology that we miss the big picture. For example, some of the calamities which befall mankind are very complex combinations of atmospheric phenomena. Do you see how it would be counterproductive to try to apprehend every detail of events John describes and miss the big picture of divine retribution?

4. Do you understand the importance of the times in which the Apocalypse was set as we try to ascertain how to interpret it for today? Do you see why it would be a good thing to know some basic history of the times during the first century AD? Most of us don't have a very good foundation for this. How might we pick up some historical perspective?

5. Hendriksen suggests that it is important to understand how the Apocalypse fits with the rest of Scripture. How is your background here? Are you a rookie? Or have you been boning up on Scripture for years so that you have a pretty good background with which to work? Does this give you some incentive to get in the Word—perhaps to read through the book?

6. Ultimately, God is the Author of the Revelation. If Hendriksen is correct and this book is actually God's plan for His creation, don't you think it might be a good idea to be familiar with its contents?

THE REVELATION
Overview

Key Verses

- The Revelation of Jesus Christ, which God gave Him to show to His bond-servants, the things which must soon take place; and He sent and communicated it by His angel to His bond-servant John, who testified to the word of God and to the testimony of Jesus Christ, even to all that he saw. Revelation 1:1
- When I saw Him, I fell at His feet like a dead man. And He placed His right hand on me, saying, "Do not be afraid; I am the first and the last, and the living One; and I was dead, and behold, I am alive forevermore, and I have the keys of death and of Hades. Therefore write the things which you have seen, and the things which are, and the things which will take place after these things." Revelation 1:17-20

Major Divisions of The Revelation

- See the Meta Story of History outline, page 146.
- See the bookchart of "The Revelation."
- See the material on "Symbols in Revelation."
- See the map of "Seven Churches of Revelation."

Application

1. A bookchart of a book of the Bible can give one a quick overview of the material covered in the book. Was the bookchart included in the notes helpful to you in over-viewing The Revelation?
2. In studying and applying God's word, one needs to be a historian and a geographer. Has our focus on geographical locations been helpful? Do you think it would be useful to make frequent reference to maps in studying the Word?

3. We have the Romans to thank for the fact that travel was possible during the period of The Revelation. We also have them to thank for the persecution that prompted Jesus to give His Revelation to John so that we might be warned of "the things to come." Do you have a good idea now of the historical and geographical setting of The Revelation?

4. Many people put off studying The Revelation because they are afraid they may not understand everything the book reveals. Of course, that is a valid concern, but not adequate to prevent us from trying to understand what Jesus revealed to John. Are you ready to roll up your sleeves and push on?

5. Of course, one of the biggest challenges in understanding this book is the symbolism used to communicate the message. You will probably want to mark the pages which give our take on the symbols so you can return to the definitions from time to time. Did you find the summary of symbolism helpful? Are you ready now to tackle this challenging book?

REVELATION
Book Chart

Part I: The Struggle on Earth (1-11)

Section	Chapter	Content
Seven Lampstands	1	1-3 Introduction
		4-7 Salutation
		8 Declaration
		9-20 Seven Lampstands
	2	1-7 Message to Ephesus
		8-11 Message to Smyrna
		12-17 Message to Pergamum
		12-17 Message to Thyatira
	3	1-6 Message to Sardis
		7-13 Message to Philadelphia
		14-22 Message to Laodicea
Seven Seals	4	1-11 The Scene in Heaven
	5	1-12 The Scroll with Seals
	6	1-2 The First Seal. The White Horse
		3-4 The Second Seal. The Red Horse
		5-6 The Third Seal. The Black Horse
		7-8 The Fourth Seal. The Ashen Horse
		9-11 The Fifth Seal. The Martyrs
		12-17 The Sixth Seal. The Final Judgment
	7	1-8 The Bond-servants of God. 144,000
		9-17 The Church Triumphant
Seven Trumpets	8	1-2 The Seventh Seal. Seven Angels
		3-5 The Prayers of the Saints
		6 Preparation for Trumpets
		7 The First Trumpet. Hail and Fire
		8-9 The Second Trumpet. The Mountain
		10-11 The Third Trumpet. The Star
		12-13 The Fourth Trumpet. Heavenly Bodies

REVELATION
Book Chart

Part I (Continued)			Part II: The Cosmic Struggle (12-22)		
Seven Trumpets (Continued)			The Woman, the Child, the Dragon		Seven Bowls
Chapter					
9	10	11	12	13	14	15	16

Chapter 9
- 1-11 The Fifth Trumpet. Satan Fallen
- 12 The First Woe. Locusts
- 13-21 The Sixth Trumpet. Four Angels

Chapter 10
- 1-11 The Word of God. The Angel

Chapter 11
- 1-2 The Temple of God
- 3-13 The Two Witnesses
- 14 The Second Woe. An Earthquake. The Third Woe
- 15-18 The Seventh Trumpet. Voices in Heaven
- 19 The Sanctuary of God

Chapter 12
- 1-6 The Woman, the Child, the Dragon
- 7-12 The Dragon Thrown Down
- 13-17 The Dragon's Final Assault

Chapter 13
- 1-10 The Beast from the Sea
- 11-18 The Beast from the Earth

Chapter 14
- 1-5 The Lamb and His Flock
- 6-7 Announcement of Judgment
- 8 Announcement of Defeat
- 9-12A Warning
- 13A Blessing
- 14-16 Harvesting the Earth
- 17-20 Harvesting the Clusters

Chapter 15
- 1-4 A Sea of Glass
- 5-8 The Sanctuary of God

Chapter 16
- 1-2 The First Bowl. Malignant Sores
- 3 The Second Bowl. Blood in the Sea
- 4-7 The Third Bowl. Blood in Rivers
- 8-9 The Fourth Bowl. Fierce Heat
- 10-11 The Fifth Bowl. Darkness
- 11-16 The Sixth Bowl. Unclean Spirits
- 17-21 The Seventh Bowl. An Earthquake

REVELATION
Book Chart

Part II: (Continued)

	Chapter	Section
Fall of the Harlot & Beasts	17	1-18 Babylon, the Great Harlot
	18	1-3 Babylon is Fallen
		4-20 Babylon is Judged
		21-24 Babylon's Epitaph
	19	1-10 The Marriage of the Lamb
		11-16 The Coming of the King
		17-18 Armageddon Announced
		19-21 Armageddon Accomplished
Judgment of the Dragon, New Heaven, New Earth	20	1-3 The Binding of Satan
		4-6 The Reign of the Saints
		7-10 The Final Conflict
		11-15 The Great White Throne
	21	1-8 The New Heaven and the New Earth
		9-27 The New Jerusalem I
		1-8 The New Jerusalem II
	22	6-7 Authority of the Book
		8-9 Authority of the Author
		10-15 A Serious Warning
		16 Authority of Jesus
		17 An Invitation
		18-19 A Second Warning
		20 John's Response
		21 John's Benediction

THE REVELATION
Major Symbolism of the Book

The Seven Lampstands (1:13). The seven lampstands represent the seven churches of Chapters 2-3; the churches are lampstands or light-bearers.

The Scroll with Seven Seals (5:1). The scroll represents God's eternal plan; God's purpose with respect to the entire universe throughout history, and concerning all creatures in all ages and to all eternity.

The Seven Seals (5:1). The seals described primarily in Chapter 6 are symbolic of tribulation and persecution. [The seventh seal is first mentioned in 8:1.]

The First Seal: the White Horse (6:2). The white horse is symbolic of the Lord Jesus Christ riding forth to conquer.

The Second Seal: the Red Horse (6:3,4). The red horse symbolizes religious persecution resulting in martyrdom of God's children.

The Third Seal: The Black Horse (6:5,6). The black horse symbolizes religious persecution resulting in poverty and hardship for God's children.

The Fourth Seal: the Ashen Horse (6:7,8). The ashen horse is symbolic of death in the universal sense—all men and women, believers and unbelievers alike, face death.

The Fifth Seal: Martyred Souls (6:9-11). The fifth seal symbolizes the souls of all who have been martyred for their faith in God and testimony for Him.

The Sixth Seal: Heavenly Turmoil (6:12-17). The calamities described with the breaking of the sixth seal symbolize the final judgment at the end of the age.

The 144,000 (7:4). This sealed multitude symbolizes the entire Church of the old and new dispensations. The number is not to be taken literally.

The Seventh Seal: Seven Angels with Seven Trumpets (8:1,2). The trumpets symbolize warnings of impending judgment throughout the church age.

The First Trumpet: Hail and Fire (8:7). Hail and fire represent various disasters that take place on earth that warn and afflict persecutors of the Church.

The Second Trumpet: a Mountain (8:8,9). The thing like a mountain represents various maritime disasters that warn and afflict the wicked.

The Third Trumpet: Wormwood (8:10,11). The star falling represents acts of God directed at inland waters to warn and afflict.

The Fourth Trumpet: Heavenly Bodies (8:12,13). God uses cosmic disturbances to warn and afflict the wicked.

The Fifth Trumpet: a Fallen Star (9:1,2). The fallen star is symbolic of Satan who receives the key to hell to loose demons with their wicked influence and operations.

The First Woe: Locusts (9:3-12). The locusts symbolize the operations of the powers of darkness in the souls of the wicked during the present age.

The Sixth Trumpet: Four Angels (9:13-21). These four angels are evil beings intent on plunging mankind into war during the present age.

The Little Book (10:1,2). The little book (or scroll) which the angel had in his hand is symbolic of the Word of God—the gospel.

The Temple of God (11:1,2). The temple here represents the true Church—all those in whose hearts Christ dwells in the Spirit.

The Two Witnesses (11:3). These witnesses symbolize the Church militant in its missionary task in the present age.

The Second Woe: an Earthquake (11:13,14). As the earthquake in the sixth seal represented the coming Day of Judgment so also does this earthquake.

The Third Woe (11:14). The text tells us that the third woe is coming quickly, but it doesn't tell us what it is. Possibly the relegation of Satan to earth (12:9).

The Seventh Trumpet: Voices in Heaven (11:15+). The voices indicate that the full royal splendor of God's sovereignty is shortly to be revealed and opposition abolished.

The Woman (12:1). The woman clearly symbolizes the Church—the twelve starred crown symbolizes victory.

The Child (12:2). The child represents the seed of the woman and in the symbology is the Lord Jesus Christ.

The Great Red Dragon (12:3,4). The dragon symbolizes Satan (the devil); the heads speak of world dominion and the horns indicate destructive power; the stars he swept from heaven to earth represent evil demons [see Jude 6].

The Beast from the Sea [The Antichrist] (13:1). The sea represents nations and their governments; thus the Sea-Born Beast symbolizes anti-Christian government—the devil's hands.

The Beast from the Earth [The False Prophet] (13:11). The Earth-Born Beast symbolizes anti-Christian religion and anti-Christian wisdom—the devil's mind.

The Vine of the Earth (14:18). The vine represents the entire multitude of evil men; its grapes are individual unbelievers.

The Sea of Glass Mixed with Fire (15:1,2). The sea symbolizes God's transparent righteousness revealed in judgments upon the wicked.

The Sanctuary Filled with Smoke (15:5-8). The sanctuary symbolizes the full and thorough operation of God's holy anger.

The Bowls of Gold Full of the Wrath of God (15:7). The bowls are of gold as they are used in the service of God; they are full, indicating the fierceness and unmitigated character of God's wrath.

The First Bowl: Malignant Sores (16:1,2). The sores represent vicious incurable diseases by which unbelievers are delivered into hell.

The Second Bowl: Blood in the Sea (16:3). Often the wicked are delivered into hell by maritime disasters represented by blood in the sea.

The Third Bowl: Blood in Rivers (16:4-7). Pollution of water sources and flooding of rivers are often the means by which the impenitent are punished.

The Fourth Bowl: Fierce Heat (16:8,9). Drought and elevated temperatures are sometimes the vehicles with which God afflicts wicked men.

The Fifth Bowl: Darkness (16:10,11). When evil governments collapse or decline, the wicked who are citizens usually suffer.

The Sixth Bowl: Unclean Spirits (16:12-16). The dragon, the beast, and the false prophet instigate many battles in which believers and unbelievers are killed and suffer.

The Seventh Bowl: An Earthquake (16:17-21). As in the case of the seventh seal and the seventh trumpet, the seventh bowl signifies that final judgment is imminent.

Babylon, the Great Harlot (17:1+). Babylon symbolizes a harlot—anything that allures, tempts, seduces, and draws people away from God.

The Marriage of the Lamb (19:7). The occasion of Jesus coming in heaven to take for Himself His bride, the Church.

Armageddon [Har-Magedon] (19:17-21). The symbol of every battle when believers are oppressed; also the final battle in which Christ appears on clouds of glory to rescue His people.

The Great White Throne (20:11-15). The great white throne is the judgment seat of Christ. All individuals who ever lived on earth will appear before this throne.

The New Heaven and the New Earth (21:1). Genesis tells us that God created heaven and earth; the Revelation describes a new heaven and earth—a gloriously rejuvenated heaven and earth.

The New Jerusalem (21:2). The New Jerusalem is clearly the Church of the Lord Jesus Christ—the Bride of Christ.

The Seven Churches of the Revelation

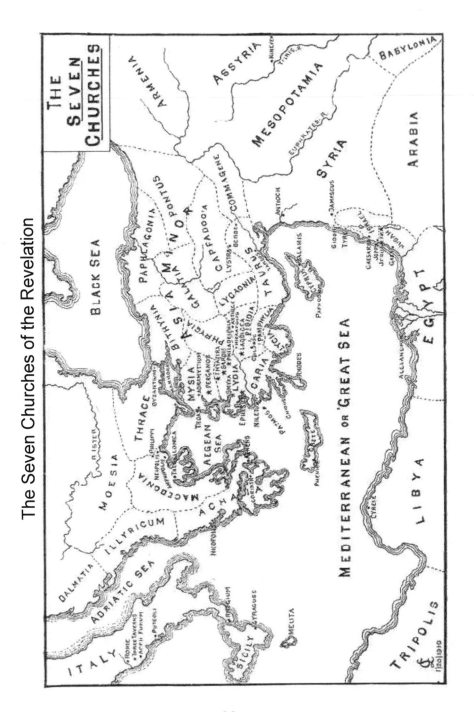

THE REVELATION
Chapter 1

The Introduction. Revelation 1:1-3

- Title. The Revelation of Jesus Christ.
  - God's plan for His creation.
    - For the history of the world.
    - Of things which will occur soon.
  - Given through John to the church.
- Origin and Transmission.
  - God.
  - Jesus.
  - An angel.
  - John.
  - The reader.
  - The hearer.

The Salutation. Revelation 1:4-6

- Addressees. The Seven Churches.
- Blessing.
  - Grace.
  - Peace.
- Authors.
  - God. Who was, and is, and is to come.
  - The Holy Spirit. The seven spirits.
  - Christ.
    - The faithful witness.
    - The first-born from the dead.
    - The ruler of earthly kings.
    - The One who loves believers.
    - The One whose blood releases.

Announcement of Christ's Second Coming. Revelation 1:7

Christ's Self-Designation. Revelation 1:8

- Alpha and Omega.
- Perfect Revelation.

John's Commission. Revelation 1:9-11

- John's Situation.
  - His position.
    - A fellow believer (brother).
    - A partaker of tribulation.
  - His location.
    - On the Isle of Patmos.
    - On the Lord's Day.
    - In the Spirit.
- John's Charge.
  - Write in a book what you see.
  - Send it to the seven churches.

John's Vision of Jesus Christ. Revelation 1:12-16

- Jesus—His Actions.
  - Speaking to John.
  - Standing among lampstands.
- Jesus—His Appearance.
  - His dress.
    - A long robe.
    - A golden belt.
  - His person.
    - Hair like snow.
    - Eyes like fire.
    - Feet like bronze.
    - Voice like waters.
    - Face like the sun.
  - His accoutrements.
    - Seven stars in His right hand.
    - Two-edged sword from His mouth.

"The entire picture, taken as a whole, is symbolical of Christ, the Holy One, coming to purge His churches, and to punish those who are persecuting His elect."

John's Interaction with Jesus. Revelation 1:17-20

- John's Reaction: Prostration.
- Jesus' Assurances.
  - He laid His hand on John.
  - He allays John's fears.
  - He identifies Himself.
    - I am the first and last.
    - I am the living One.
    - I am the crucified One.
    - I am the eternal One.
    - I have the keys of death and Hades.
- Jesus' Instructions.
  - Write.
    - Things you have seen.
    - Things which are.
    - Things which will take place
  - Understand.
    - Seven stars are the ministers of the churches.
    - Seven lampstands are the seven churches.

Applications

1. We often read through the verses of Chapter 1 so hurriedly that we miss the significance of the transmission: from God to Jesus to the angel to John to Scripture. What does this process say to you about the importance of this book?
2. Assuming John was twenty or so when he began following Jesus in about 27 AD, at the time of this vision he would have been in his eighties—certainly an old man by any measure. What does this say to you about your usefulness to Jesus?
3. The detail John gives about his vision of Jesus is impressive. It has a ring of truth about it. Hendriksen explains it as a picture

of Christ coming to purge His churches and to punish those who persecute believers. Does John's description fit Hendriksen's explanation? Elaborate.

4. John's response to his encounter with Jesus was to fall prostrate on his face—not a bad move when face to face with the living God. Do you recognize Jesus as the God of all creation? Do you worship at His feet?

5. How like Jesus to put His hand on John (his shoulder I imagine) to reassure him. As believers in Christ we have nothing to fear from Him; He is our Brother and our Advocate with the Father. We should worship Him—holding Him in awe—but we should not fear Him. Do you agree?

6. Aren't you glad that Jesus gave us this view of God's purposes in His creation? Does this introduction challenge you to roll up your sleeves and study this book?

Note. Be sure to make frequent reference to the chart on page 147 as you read through the letters to the seven churches in Chapters 2 and 3.

THE REVELATION
Chapter 2

The Message to the Church at Ephesus. Revelation 2:1-7

- Background.
  - Location.
    - On the western coast of Asia Minor.
    - Where Cayster River flows into Aegean.
    - ~250 miles due east by sea from Athens.
  - History.
    - City founded in 10th century BC.
    - City had a distinguished history.
    - Church established by Paul (52AD).
    - Church led by Aquila and Priscilla (54-57AD).
    - Church led by Paul (~54-57AD).
    - Paul's letter to Ephesus from Rome (61AD).
    - Church led by John (~65-95AD).
  - Distinctives.
    - Beautiful and prosperous city.
    - Temple of Diana (Artemis).
    - Deep water harbor.
    - Good highway access.
- Salutation: To the Angel of the Church in Ephesus.
- Self-Designation.
  - The One who holds the seven stars in His right hand.
  - The One who walks among the seven lampstands.
- Commendation.
  - Your deeds, your work and perseverance.
  - You cannot endure evil men.
  - You have tested apostles and found them false.
  - You have endured and not grown weary.
  - You hate the works of the Nicolaitans.
- Condemnation. You have left your first love.
- Exhortation.
  - Remember from where you have fallen.
  - Repent and do the deeds you first did.

- Warning: I will remove your lampstand. (Fulfilled)
- Promise.
  - He who overcomes...
  - Will eat of the tree of life.
- Admonition.
  - He who has ears let him hear...
  - What the Spirit says to the churches.

Applications

1. When Jesus speaks people should listen. Jesus is careful to identify Himself in this first letter so that the readers will know who the author of the letter is. Where have you heard this description of Jesus before? Do you think there can be any ambiguity as to whom these attributes refer?
2. The Ephesians have a pretty long list of good deeds for which Jesus commends them. Yet Jesus condemns them for losing their first love. What does He mean by this? This reminds us somewhat of those who are working hard for salvation, without faith in the One who gives salvation. Doesn't it? Discuss.
3. Jesus admonishes the Ephesians to hear the messages to the churches—that is, to all seven of the churches. Can we take it from this that all seven of the messages are important to us today as His followers? Does this motivate you to dig into the messages to see how they apply to us today?
4. Jesus instructs the Ephesian believers "to remember from where you have fallen." What does He mean by this? Is this a good thing? It is always good to look back; but when we do, we want to see progress, not falling away. What are some of the ways we can fall away? What are some ways we should be progressing?
5. What does Jesus mean by "he who overcomes?" Would you classify yourself as an overcomer? Why or why not? If not, what do you need to change so that you would deserve His commendation in this respect? What does it mean to "eat of the tree of life?"

6. Jesus directs John to admonish the reader to hear what the Spirit says to the churches. Are you beginning to feel that with a little digging we can unlock some of the secrets of this wonderful book? Aren't you glad that we are making the effort? Is Revelation 1:3 beginning to come to pass for you?

The Message to the Church at Smyrna. Revelation 2:8-11

- Background.
  - Location.
    - Commercial port on the Aegean Sea.
    - Near the ruins of an ancient Greek colony.
    - 35 miles north of Ephesus.
  - History.
    - City was built by the Greeks (3rd century BC).
    - Church founded by Paul (53-56AD).
    - Church led by Polycarp (d. 155AD), a disciple of John.
  - Distinctives.
    - "First City of Asia" in beauty.
    - Known for loyalty to the Romans.
    - 100,000 population in NT times.
- Salutation: To the Angel of the Church in Smyrna.
- Self-Designation.
  - The first and last who was dead.
  - The One who has come to life.
- Commendation.
  - Your tribulation and poverty.
  - Your enemy's blasphemy.
- Condemnation. None.
- Exhortation.
  - Do not fear the future.
  - Be faithful unto death.
- Warning.
  - Satan will throw some of you into prison.
  - You will be tested and face tribulation for ten days.
- Promise.
  - He who overcomes...

- Shall not be hurt by death.
- I will give the crown of life.
- Admonition.
  - He who has ears let him hear...
  - What the Spirit says to the churches.

Applications

1. What do you think about the way Jesus described Himself to the Church in Smyrna? Is it pretty clear to whom these characterizations apply? Have you ever received a message from Jesus? Be careful how you answer; this is a trick question. (Hint: the answer is "yes.") Explain.
2. Why is it important that Jesus knew that the Jews in Smyrna were particularly hostile toward Christians? Do you think Jesus knows what you are up against in life? At home? At the office? In the neighborhood? Is it reassuring to you to know that He knows your challenges? Do we have it pretty easy compared to others? Elaborate.
3. It doesn't bode well when Jesus exhorts the Christians of Smyrna to "be faithful until death." One gets the impression that death may be sooner rather than later. What would you conclude if you received such a message? Of course, we never know how long we have to live. One of my prayers is to be able to finish strong. What about you?
4. Jesus informs the Smyrna believers that some of them will go to prison for testing. What does He mean by this? Have you ever undergone testing? Could you describe the testing? What about the outcome? Is testing always a bad thing? Can you describe some outcomes of testing that are good?
5. What does Jesus mean by "the crown of life?" What does He mean by "the second death?" Is this like the puzzlement Nicodemus felt over being born again (John 3)? Are you beginning to see how important it is for us to be "more than conquerors?"

The Message to the Church at Pergamum. Revelation 2:12-17

- Background.
  - Location.
    - About 50 miles due north of Smyrna.
    - About 10 miles east of the Aegean Sea.
    - Built on a conical hill 1,000' above valley.
  - History.
    - City dates to Alexander the Great (~300BC).
    - City was made the provincial capital by Romans.
    - Nothing apart from this passage is known of the church.
  - Distinctives.
    - Temple for worship of Augustus Caesar (29BC).
    - Temple of Dionysus (Bacchus), the god of wine.
    - The Altar of Zeus (exhibited at Pergamum Museum in Berlin).
    - Temple of Asklepion, the god of medicine (4th century BC).
    - Library (200,000 volumes) second only to Alexandria, Egypt.
    - Parchment was first developed in Pergamum.
- Salutation: To the Angel of the Church in Pergamum.
- Self-Designation: The One Who Has the Sharp Two-edged Sword.
- Commendation.
  - You live where Satan's throne is.
  - You held fast to My name.
  - You did not deny me even when Antipas was killed.
- Condemnation.
  - Some hold to the teaching of Balaam.
  - Some hold to the teaching of the Nicolaitans.
- Exhortation: Repent of these things.
- Warning:
  - I will come to you quickly.
  - I will make war against them.
- Promise.
  - He who overcomes...

-    I will give hidden manna.
-    I will give a white stone.
  - ▪ Identification of the wearer?
  - ▪ Identification of Christ?
- Admonition.
  - He who has ears let him hear...
  - What the Spirit says to the church<u>e</u>s.

Applications

1. Hendriksen suggests that Christ's reference to the two-edged sword in this message is not to be understood as the Bible, but of His coming to make war against the members of the church who continued in their worldly practices—participation in idol worship and feasts. What do you think of this interpretation?

2. Jesus recognized that Pergamum was a tough place for believers to live because of all the temples and pagan worship in the city. What about us? Is your city a tough place for believers? Does Jesus understand the temptations of living in affluent places? Will He make allowances for us on this account?

3. It is very common for people today even as in John's time to embrace incorrect doctrine. The "Prosperity Gospel" (Name It and Claim It) is probably the most egregious example in our own times, but there are certainly others. Can you cite some examples? Does Jesus take this seriously? Should we?

4. If someone were to confront you in a nice way concerning some faulty doctrine you held, what would you do? Would you listen? Would you automatically conclude they were right? Do you understand why it is so important that we are continually in the Scriptures (see Acts 17:10,11)?

5. Some people wear large crosses around their necks to identify themselves as Christians. Some wear cross lapel pins. What do you think of such practices? Do you employ any external symbols to let others know of your relationship with Jesus? Would you share this?

The Message to the Church at Thyatira. Revelation 2:18-29

- Background.
  - Location.
    - About 35 miles southeast of Pergamum.
    - On the south bank of the Lycus River.
  - History.
    - City was refounded by Seleucus Nicator (~300BC).
    - The name means "the castle of Thya."
    - Paul may have preached here (Acts 19:10).
    - Home of Lydia, a dealer of purple cloth (Acts 16:13+)
    - Nothing is known of the church in Thyatira.
  - Distinctives.
    - Important trade center especially for textiles.
    - Noted for trade guilds—a requirement for artisans.
    - Dyers made use of the madder root for purple dye.
    - Cultic center to Apollo, the sun god.
    - Temple of Sambethe; prophetess referred to as Jezebel.
    - Modern name of the city is Akhisar (White Castle).
- Salutation: To the Angel of the Church in Thyatira.
- Self-Designation:
  - The Son of God who has eyes like a flame of fire.
  - The Son of God whose feet are like burnished bronze.
- Commendation.
  - Your love, service, and perseverance.
  - Your deeds are increasing with time.
- Condemnation.
  - Some tolerate the prophetess (Jezebel).
    - Committing acts of immorality.
    - Eating food sacrificed to idols.
  - Others haven't strayed.
    - You are innocent of immorality.
    - You are spared additional burdens.
- Exhortation: Unless There is Repentance:
  - I will afflict her (Jezebel).
  - I will bring tribulation to her followers.
  - I will kill her children with pestilence.

41

- I am He who searches minds and hearts.
- I reward according to your deeds.
- Warning: Hold fast.
- Promise.
  - He who overcomes…
  - I will give authority over the nations.
  - I will give the morning star.
- Admonition.
  - He who has ears let him hear…
  - What the Spirit says to the churches.

Applications

1. Thyatira was the center of worship of the sun god Apollo. Do you think it is a coincidence that Jesus describes Himself to members of the church there as "the Son of God with eyes like a flame of fire?" Do you see the irony of this description? How often do we ourselves worship some counterfeit Jesus—similar but not the same?

2. In all probability, Lydia, the seller of purple cloth from Thyatira who trusted Christ under Paul's teaching at Philippi, was instrumental in starting the church at Thyatira. The connection is too obvious to ignore. Has God ever used you to begin a work in some way? Is He using you to sustain a work of His in any way?

3. To say that someone's good deeds are increasing is to notice that they are more and more engaged in doing good. The trend is definitely right. What about you? If we were to examine your calendar for the last several years, would we see a positive trend in your involvement in Kingdom work?

4. If you were a tradesperson in Thyatira, how successful do you think you might have been had you not belonged to the local trade guild (union)? Since guild members were expected to participate in the feasts and orgies dedicated to their patron god or goddess, there was a huge moral conflict. Any modern day parallels?

5. In this passage, Jesus says, "I will give to each one of you according to your deeds." In Hebrews 10:17, He says, "Their sins and lawless deeds I will remember no more." Is there a contradiction here? How would you explain this to a friend who was struggling with guilt? (Hint: one expression relates to unbelievers the other to believers.)

THE REVELATION
Chapter 3

The Message to the Church at Sardis. Revelation 3:1-6

- Background.
    - Location.
        - 60 miles inland from Ephesus and Smyrna.
        - On the northern slope of Mt. Tmolus.
        - Pactolus River served as a moat for the city.
    - History.
        - One of the oldest cities of Asia Minor.
        - Important to Medes, Persians, and Greeks.
        - Given independence by Alexander (335BC).
        - Destroyed by an earthquake in 17AD.
        - Never regained its former prominence.
    - Distinctives.
        - City was noted for its fruits and wool.
        - Temple of the goddess Cybele (Artemis).
        - Wealthy from gold found in its river.
        - Very large and prosperous Jewish segment.
        - Largest Jewish synagogue outside Palestine.
- Salutation: To the Angel of the Church in Sardis.
- Self-Designation.
    - He who has the seven Spirits.
    - He who has the seven stars.
- Commendation.
    - Your deeds.
    - Your name.
        - Indicates you are alive.
        - But you really are dead.
- Condemnation.
    - Most of you.
        - Have soiled your garments.
        - Are therefore dead to Me.
    - A few of you.
        - Have not soiled your garments.

- Will therefore walk with Me.
- Exhortation.
  - Wake up and strengthen your work.
  - Remember what you have received.
  - Repent of your worldliness.
- Warning: I will come to you unannounced.
- Promise.
  - He who overcomes...
  - Shall wear white garments.
  - His name:
    - Will not be erased from the book of life.
    - Will be confessed before the Father.
- Admonition.
  - He who has ears let him hear...
  - What the Spirit says to the churche̲s̲.

Applications

1. Jesus identifies Himself to the Church of Sardis as the One who has the seven Spirits and the seven stars. This may be taken as One who wishes to breathe life (Spirits) into a church that is dying. Have you ever been in a dying church? It is not a pleasant place to be. What did/should you do?

2. The central focus of the message to Sardis is soiled clothing—another way of identifying worldliness. Worldliness is certainly a problem in our day and time—we call it materialism or conformity. This reminds us of Paul's admonition in Romans 12:1,2. Comments?

3. Jesus admonishes the believers in Sardis to "wake up and remember." There is a sense in which we are sometimes lulled into spiritual stupor—we slide into attachments with the world. This is basically what Robert Bork was addressing in his book *Slouching toward Gommorah*. Can you elaborate?

4. Jesus commends "a few" of the people for not having soiled their clothing. What about you? If Jesus returned to earth today, would He find you attached to the world or would He

find you with a proper attitude toward the things of the world in relation to the things of Christ?

5. White garments symbolize purity. Jesus suggests that we must be pure to walk or have fellowship with Him. He also mentions the "book of life." How does one maintain purity of character in the midst of a fallen world? Is your name permanently recorded in the book of life?

6. Even though the largest Jewish population outside of Palestine was located in Sardis, they are not directly mentioned in the letter. Why do you suppose this is so? Do you think there was hostility from the Jews toward the Christians of the city? Does the fact that their works were incomplete have any bearing?

The Message to the Church at Philadelphia. Revelation 3:7-13

- Background.
  - Location.
    - ~100 miles east of Smyrna; 26 miles from Sardis.
    - On a terrace 650 feet above sea level.
    - Situated in front of volcanic cliffs.
    - Fertile plains beyond the cliffs.
  - History.
    - City was founded in 189 BC.
    - Named for brother of the king of Lydia.
    - Also called Decapolis—one of the 10 cities of the plains.
    - Destroyed by an earthquake in 17AD.
  - Distinctives.
    - Called "Little Athens" for temples and public buildings.
    - Became a center of the wine industry in the region.
    - Chief deity was Dionysus (Bacchus), the god of wine.
- Salutation: To the Angel of the Church in Philadelphia.
- Self-Designation.
  - He who is holy and true.
  - He who has the key of David:
    - Who opens and no one will shut.
    - Who shuts and no one opens.

- Commendation.
  - I know your deeds.
  - I put before you an open door, because:
    - You have a little power.
    - You have kept My word.
    - You have not denied My name.
- Condemnation. None.
- Exhortation. Hold fast what you have.
- Warning. To those of the Synagogue of Satan:
  - I will make them bow at your feet, so that...
  - They will know I have loved you.
- Promise.
  - Because...
    - You have persevered.
    - I will keep you from testing.
      - Which is about to come.
      - Which men will endure.
  - He who overcomes...
    - He will be a pillar in the temple.
    - He will not leave the temple.
    - He will have the name of God written on him.
    - He will have the name of God's city written on him.
- Admonition.
  - He who has ears let him hear...
  - What the Spirit says to the churches.

Applications

1. Jesus describes Himself in this message as He who is holy and true. Only God who is holy can also be true. He will always keep His promises; He is always faithful to His word; He will never stop loving us. Does God's faithfulness challenge you to also be faithful to those whom you love?
2. The Church in Philadelphia is characterized as having "a little power." Yet God says He will give it the "key of David," symbolizing the highest authority in His Kingdom. Individuals and organizations which appear weak in the eyes of the world

can accomplish much if energized by God's power. Can you give some examples?

3. God had some special plans for the Jews in Philadelphia—to bow at the feet of the believers there to demonstrate that God loved them. While we have no historical record that this happened in John's time, it is significant that the Jews have suffered 2000 years of persecution while Christians have generally prospered. Comment.

4. Jesus makes some wonderful promises to the Philadelphia believers—one promise was that He would keep them from testing. God apparently had already tested these believers and they passed the test—they persevered. Perhaps you have lived through some tough times—financially, health-wise, etc. Did you pass the test? Explain.

5. Philadelphia and Smyrna are the only two churches of the seven which Jesus doesn't condemn. Philadelphia was apparently small and the one at Smyrna was poor and poverty smitten. If we had picked one of the churches to join based on externals, we probably would have picked one of the others. What does this say about small and poor?

The Message to the Church at Laodicea. Revelation 3:14-22.

- Background.
  - Location.
    - About 100 miles east of Ephesus.
    - A few miles from Colossae.
    - At the junction of several important highways.
  - History.
    - Founded by Antiochus II (~260BC).
    - Named for Antiochus' wife, Laodice.
    - Populated with Syrians and Jews from Babylon.
    - Paul's letter to the Colossians sent here (Colossians 4:15,16).
    - Almost destroyed by an earthquake in 66AD.
  - Distinctives.
    - A great and wealthy center of industry and commerce.

48

- - Especially famous for fine black wool.
  - Phrygian powder for the eyes manufactured here.
  - Nearby Hierapolis was popular for spas and water.
  - Jews migrated from Palestine for the wines (60sAD).
- Salutation: To the Angel of the Church in Laodicea.
- Self-Designation:
  - The Amen, the faithful and true Witness.
  - The Beginning of the creation of God.
- Commendation. None.
- Condemnation.
  - Your devotion:
    - Neither hot nor cold.
    - You are lukewarm.
  - You think (say):
    - I am rich and wealthy.
    - I have need of nothing.
  - You do not know:
    - You are wretched and miserable.
    - You are poor, blind, and naked.
- Exhortation.
  - Repent. Be zealous.
  - Buy:
    - Refined gold, that you may be rich.
    - White garments, that you may be clothed.
    - Eye-salve, that you may see.
  - Open:
    - I stand at the door and knock.
    - I will come in, if I'm invited.
    - I will (dine) fellowship with you.
- Warning:
  - Those I love, I reprove and discipline.
  - Those who are lukewarm, I will spew out.
- Promise.
  - He who overcomes will sit on a throne with Me.
  - As I overcame and sit on a throne with God.
- Admonition.
  - He who has ears let him hear...

49

- What the Spirit says to the churches.

Applications

1. Jesus identifies Himself to the Laodiceans as "the faithful and true witness." What is to be done with a witness who is faithful and true? The Laodiceans had already benefited from the witness of the Apostle Paul, apparently to no avail. Now they hear from "the Beginning of creation." Ought they to have listened? Ought we?

2. The Church of Laodicea was the only one of the seven for which Jesus has nothing to commend. This is a very sad and serious state. Is the situation hopeless? Why or why not (no speculation)? The answer is one word—it starts with the letter "z." Do you think this is good advice for us as individuals. For churches?

3. The principle problem with the Church of Laodicea was their lukewarm devotion to Christ. What about us? Could Jesus point His finger at us and say, "This applies to you as well?" What are some symptoms of being lukewarm? What is the solution? What should we do about half-hearted commitment?

4. Isn't it interesting that Jesus would prescribe eye-salve which was manufactured in Laodicea for their spiritual blindness? Of course, He wasn't speaking about literal eye-salve, but the balm of God's Spirit who allows us to see ourselves as we really are through His convicting work in our lives.

5. Here is a church of which Jesus has nothing good to say. In fact, He was ready to spew them from His mouth—He was thoroughly disgusted with them. And yet, He goes on to express His love for them which He suggests is evidenced by the fact that He is willing to discipline them rather than casting them aside. Aren't we glad He loves us?

6. In closing, we need to ensure that we understand the following: "The sevenfold condition of these churches actually existed at the time of John. It exists today. It has existed during the entire intervening period. These seven churches almost certainly

50

represent the entire Church during the entire church age." Do you understand this?

CHAPTERS 2 AND 3
Comparative Note

Because the letters to the seven churches are not predictive, they are not controversial except with respect to their historical interpretation. Some adherents of the historicist and futurist schools of interpretation see certain parallels between the individual letters and successive periods of church history, from John's day to the second coming. They conclude that the seven letters present a panorama of the Church Age as follows:

- Ephesus is said to describe the church during the apostolic age from the ascension until about (100AD).
- Smyrna represents the church suffering persecution under the Roman emperors from about 100AD until 313.
- Pergamum is a church compromised with carnality and false doctrine as the church was from Constantine until the rise of the papacy in 500.
- Thyatira is seen as the papal church until the Reformation, covering the period from 500 to 1500.
- Sardis represents the church during the Reformation from 1500 to 1700. Of course, those of the reformed view object as Sardis was a dead church.
- Philadelphia is construed to be the church which experienced a resurgence of missionary activity from 1700 until the present.
- Laodicea which Jesus condemned for being lukewarm is likened to the liberal churches of modern times.

Those who criticize this position say that the entire church of any particular period of history can hardly be regarded as a homogeneous entity that fits the description of a given letter. Furthermore since the Reformation, different types of churches exist side by side, and, thus, should not be lumped together for purposes of classification.

THE SEVEN SEALS
Comparative Note

Beginning in Chapter 4 and continuing through Chapter 19, we have widely differing interpretations of the events of Revelation. We will try to give brief comparative notes, section by section, as we proceed through the book. As we consider Chapters 4-7, we need to answer the following questions:

- What events do the mysterious scroll and its unsealing represent?
- When do these events occur relative to John's vision and the church age?

As we have noted there are four major ways of interpreting the book.

Historicist Approach

- The unsealing of the scroll represents the beginning of the fall of the Roman Empire.
- The sequence of the seven seals can thus be viewed as follows:
  - The decline of the Empire begins with the reign of Domitian (died 96 AD).
  - The Empire collapsed with invasions of Goths and Vandals (4th-5th centuries).

Preterist Approach

- The unsealing of the scroll represents the judgment of God upon Jerusalem (66-70AD).
- The four horsemen represent the Roman invasion (66AD) bringing bloodshed, civil war, famine, death, and finally destruction of Jerusalem.

Futurist Approach

- The unsealing of the scroll represents the Rapture of the Church and the beginning of the Great Tribulation.

- In the end times, the Antichrist rides forth conquering on the white horse; war, famine, and cosmic disturbances (possibly nuclear) follow.

Spiritual Approach

- The scroll and its unsealing represent God's dealings with mankind, seen in cycles of war, martyrdom, and judgment recurring repeatedly throughout history.
- The visions underscore God's sovereignty in the rise and fall of earthly kingdoms and His protection of the saints in the midst of political upheavals.
- There is no attempt made to associate these experiences to specific historical events.

THE REVELATION
Chapter 4

The Setting Described. Revelation 4:1-2a

- John's Experience.
  - He looked and saw.
    - A door in heaven.
    - Standing open.
  - He listened and heard.
    - The first voice.
    - As a trumpet.
  - He was shown and related.
- John's Attitude. In the Spirit.

The Scene in Heaven. Revelation 4:2b-8a

- God on His Throne.
  - God's appearance.
    - Like jasper.
    - Like sardius.
  - God's aura.
    - Like a rainbow.
    - Like an emerald.
  - Around the throne.
    - Flashes of lightening.
    - Peals of thunder.
  - Before the throne.
    - Seven lamps of fire which are:
    - Seven Spirits of God.
    - A sea of glass like crystal.
- The Twenty-four Elders. See pages 148,149.
  - Their thrones arrayed.
  - Their persons attired:
    - White garments.
    - Golden crowns.

- The Four Living Creatures. See pages 148,149.
  - Common attributes.
    - Full of eyes.
    - Six wings.
  - Distinctive features.
    - One like a lion.
    - One like a calf.
    - One like a man.
    - One like an eagle.

The Action in Heaven. Revelation 4:8b-11.

- The Four Living Creatures.
  - Unceasing praise.
  - Unambiguous message.
    - "God is Holy."
    - "God is eternal."
- The Twenty-four Elders.
  - Worship God.
    - Prostrate before Him.
    - Casting crowns to Him.
  - Praise God.
    - "God is worthy."
    - "God is the creator."
      - Of all things.
      - By His will.

Applications

1. In describing this episode, John informs his readers that he was "in the spirit." When one is consistently walking in the Spirit as we are commanded to in Galatians 5:16 and Ephesians 5:18 (and many other places in Scripture), we can expect to be encountering God. How are you doing in your walk in the Spirit?
2. John describes for us the scene in heaven placing God on a throne in the midst of the elders and the living creatures.

Hendriksen suggests that the throne is symbolic rather than literal. Since we have only several glimpses of heaven in Scripture (Job 1, Isaiah 6, and Ezekiel 1) we can't be certain on this point. Give arguments for both sides.

3. The main picture being communicated here is that God is ruling at all times over His creation. A throne represents the seat of government—thus in John's vision he sees God firmly in control even though the forces of evil are raging on planet Earth. Does understanding this central message encourage you? Why or why not?

4. John describes his vision of God by likening Him to precious stones—jasper, sardius, and emeralds. Why would John do this? Jesus tells us in John 4:24, "God is spirit; and those who worship Him must worship in spirit and truth." Does this statement help you answer the question?

5. Some commentators think the jasper (clear), sardius (red), and emerald (green) represent God's holiness, wrath and mercy (see Ezekiel 28:17-20). They suggest that the image being communicated here is that after God's holiness prompts His wrath in the form of judgments on His creation, mercy is forthcoming. What say you?

6. Two possible interpretations of the twenty-four elders are: (1) The twelve Patriarchs of the Old Testament and the twelve Apostles of the New Testament or (2) The Church of the old and new dispensation (all believers of all times). Do you see a conflict here or can these two views be harmonized.

7. The four living creatures are identical in character to the four living creatures described in Ezekiel 1. We believe they represent the cherubim—angels who guard the holy things of God. Some, including me, have recognized the similarity between the creatures and the four Gospels. Can you harmonize these two views?

THE REVELATION
Chapter 5

The Scroll. Revelation 5:1

The Search. Revelation 5:2-5

- The Angel.
  - His demeanor.
  - His question.
- The Answer. "No one!"
- John's Response. Intense Grief.
- The Elder's Intervention.
  - He spoke to John.
  - He identified a Savior.
    - The Lion of Judah.
    - The Root of David.

The Savior. Revelation 5:6-7

- The Lamb's Place.
- The Lamb's Appearance.
  - Standing as if slain.
  - Having seven horns and eyes.
- The Lamb's Action.

Applications

1. We believe the sealed scroll symbolizes God's eternal plan—
   "His purpose with respect to the entire universe throughout all
   history, and concerning all creatures in all ages to all eternity."
   If this is so, how important do you think it might be that we
   know what is written on the scroll?
2. John initially thought that there was no one in heaven worthy
   to open the scroll thereby permitting him (and us through him)
   to know God's purposes. When he realized this, he tells us that
   he "wept greatly." Was John overreacting? What might have

been your response had you been in John's place? When we neglect Scripture, leaving our Bibles in their place for days on end, isn't this somewhat the same?

3. We are told by one of the elders that the Lion of Judah (Jesus) has overcome and is thus worthy to open the scroll. What does it mean that He has overcome? Why does that qualify Him to open the scroll?

4. When Jesus took the scroll from the hand of God, that was a significant moment in history. Do you understand the significance? Can you explain what is so significant about this event? One might even liken it to a coronation. Explain.

The Song. Revelation 5:8-14

- The Creatures and Elders.
  - Their accoutrements.
    - A harp.
    - Golden bowls.
  - Their new song.
    - You are worthy to take the scroll.
    - You made men to be a kingdom.
- Angels, Creatures, and Elders.
  - Their number.
    - Myriads of myriads.
    - Thousands of thousands.
  - Their song. "The Lamb is worthy."
- Every Created Thing.
  - Their locations.
    - In heaven.
    - On earth.
    - Under the earth.
    - On the sea.
  - Their song: "To the Lamb."
- The Creatures and Elders.
  - The creatures continually say "Amen."
  - The elders fell down and worshiped.

Applications

1. One might say of this scene, "There was ecstasy in heaven." Remember when this happened—we believe at the moment of John's vision of the event. Unfortunately, we weren't privileged to be present as John was. What do you suppose your reaction might have been had you been there?
2. Let's don't miss the things Jesus is being praised for by the heavenly hosts. First, because He was slain for shedding His blood to purchase men (us) for God. What does this mean to you? It is certainly not something to be taken lightly—in fact, we ought never to get over it. What do you think?
3. Moreover, Jesus made us (believers) to be a kingdom and priests to God. We often pray, "For Thine is the Kingdom..." What does that mean? Do you ever think of yourself as a priest to God? What does that entail? How are you doing with your priestly duties?
4. The angels say, "Worthy is the Lamb that was slain to receive power and riches and wisdom and might and honor and glory and blessing." From where are these things to come? What might be your contribution? Don't you think it might be important for you to be able to participate in the ceremony?

THE REVELATION
Chapter 6

The First Seal. Revelation 6:1,2

- The Seal Broken.
  - The Lamb.
  - The Creature.
- The Seal Dispatched.
  - The white horse. See page 150.
  - The horse's rider. Jesus Christ.
    - A bow.
    - A crown.
  - The rider's mission. To conquer.

The Second Seal. Revelation 6:3,4

- The Seal Broken.
  - The Lamb.
  - The Creature.
- The Seal Dispatched.
  - The red horse. Religious persecution.
  - The horse's rider. A great sword [machaira].
  - The horse's mission.
    - To take peace from the earth.
    - To set men against one another.

The Third Seal. Revelation 6:5,6

- The Seal Broken.
  - The Lamb.
  - The Creature.
- The Seal Dispatched.
  - The black horse. Poverty.
  - The horse's rider. A pair of scales.
  - The voice [of God].
    - "A quart of wheat for a denarius..."

- "Do not harm the oil and the wine."
  - The rider's mission. Physical suffering.

The Fourth Seal. Revelation 6:7,8

- The Seal Broken.
  - The Lamb.
  - The Creature.
- The Seal Dispatched.
  - The ashen horse.
  - The horse's rider. Death.
  - The rider's attendant. Hades.
  - The rider's mission. Death.
    - By the sword (war), [rhomphaia]. See page 158.
    - By famine (hunger).
    - By pestilence (disease).
    - By wild beasts (animals).

Applications

1. Some suggest that the rider on the white horse is the Antichrist. Read John 16:33 and Revelation 3:21. Do you see why from these verses (and others) we understand the rider to be the Lord Jesus Christ?
2. Given that the rider on the white horse is Jesus, His riding out to conquer would represent the winning of souls throughout the church age. Does this remind you of the hymn "Onward Christian Soldiers?" Explain.
3. The Second and Third Seals should be taken together and represent religious persecution throughout the church age. How does religious persecution today compare with that of John's day?
4. Regarding the Third Seal as economic hardship suffered by believers throughout the church age, can you point to specific examples in history of Christians suffering economic discrimination?

5. The number of people who have died throughout the church age because of war, hunger, disease, and wild animals is staggering—probably in excess of 50 percent of the total number of people who have ever lived. Would you agree or disagree? In what sense does this represent God's judgment?

The Fifth Seal. Revelation 6:9-11

- The Seal Broken.
  - The Lamb.
  - The Martyrs.
- The Seal Delayed.
  - The Martyr's lament.
    - "How long, O Lord, holy and true?"
    - "Will You delay judgment and vengeance?"
  - The Martyr's reward.
    - A white robe.
    - A short rest.

The Sixth Seal. Revelation 6:12-17

- The Seal Broken.
  - The Lamb.
  - The Final Judgment.
- The Seal Described.
  - Cosmic disturbances. See page 155.
    - Earthquakes.
    - Sun, moon, stars.
  - Human reaction.
    - All mankind.
    - Running for cover.

Applications

1. The number of people throughout the church age who have been killed (martyred) for their faith can only be surmised. We are told that more people have been martyred in the last 100

years than in all the time since Jesus. Can you cite evidence for this?

2. It is sobering to read in this section "their brethren who were to be killed" which refers to believers who will be killed for their faith—future tense. Of course, we don't know how many will die, but the chances of any of us being martyred are pretty remote, don't you think?

3. Have you ever experienced an earthquake? Having experienced the 1964 quake in Alaska, I can attest to the fact that it is pretty scary and we were 500 miles from the epicenter. Do you think you would dive for cover in the face of widespread cosmic disturbances?

4. Verse 16 is interesting. Those who are hiding ask the mountains to hide them "from the presence of Him who sits on the throne, and from the wrath of the Lamb." How do they know God and Jesus are behind the disturbances? Why can't people see God in circumstances today?

THE REVELATION
Chapter 7

The Bondservants of God. Revelation 7:1-8

- What John Saw.
  - Four angels.
    - Standing at the four corners of the earth.
    - Waiting to harm the earth and the sea.
    - Holding back the four winds of the earth.
      - Restraining wind on the earth.
      - Restraining wind on the sea.
      - Restraining wind on the trees.
  - Another angel.
    - Ascending from the east.
    - Having the seal of God.
    - Speaking in a loud voice.
      - "Do not harm the earth or the sea..."
      - "Until we have marked the bondservants."
- What John Heard.
  - The number of bondservants: 144,000.
  - From every tribe of Israel.
    - Judah, Reuben, Gad: 12,000.
    - Asher, Naphtali, Manasseh: 12,000.
    - Simeon, Levi, Issachar: 12,000.
    - Zebulun, Joseph, Benjamin: 12,000.

The Church Triumphant. Revelation 7:9-17

- Great Multitude.
  - Their number: innumerable.
  - Their origin:
    - Every nation.
    - All tribes.
    - All races.
    - All languages.
  - Their position: Before the Lamb.

- Their accoutrements:
    - Clothed in white robes.
    - Holding palm branches.
- Their worship.
    - To God.
    - To the Lamb.
- The Heavenly Host.
    - Their number:
        - All the angels.
        - The 24 elders.
        - The living creatures.
        - All believers.
    - Their position:
        - Before the throne.
        - On their faces.
    - Their worship: To God.
        - Blessing.
        - Wisdom.
        - Honor.
        - Might.
        - Glory.
        - Thanksgiving.
        - Power.
- The Interchange.
    - Participants.
        - One of the elders.
        - The Apostle John.
    - The Dialog.
        - The questions.
            - Who are these people?
            - From where have they come?
        - John's reply. "You know."
        - The answers:
            - They have come out of the (the great) tribulation.
            - They have been cleansed by the blood of the Lamb.
            - They are before the throne of God serving Him.
            - They are all under the protection of God.
            - They shall never hunger or thirst or suffer from sun.
            - They shall be lead by the Lamb.
            - They shall have all tears wiped away.

Applications

1. Here there is a pause in the action of breaking the seals on the scroll representing the purposes of God in His creation. John watches as four angels hold back destruction that is targeted for planet earth. The reason for this delay is so that believers throughout the church age may be sealed. Are you clear on what it means to be sealed?
2. John tells us he heard the number of those who were sealed—144,000; twelve thousand from each of the twelve tribes "of the sons of Israel." Are you satisfied that the number 144,000 is symbolic and represents all believers in all times, including us who believe today?
3. Some today argue that the 144,000 symbolizes the nation of Israel. We have considered several arguments why this does not seem likely. Are you satisfied that the 144,000 is almost certainly not a symbol for Israel?
4. After this, John is enabled to see the church triumphant as it will be in eternity—in the very presence of God. John describes it as a great multitude (> 144,000), innumerable, from every nation, tribe, people, and tongue. All are standing before the throne dressed in white robes praising God. Do you have any trouble dealing with heaven as a multicultural place?
5. I had a colleague who told me that he thought he would be bored with heaven, "Just standing around all day praising God." He probably didn't need to worry, because I don't think he made it. I hope I'm wrong. What about you? Are you excited about the prospect of one day joining this heavenly throng?
6. Why does the elder (verse 13) ask John who those clothed in white robes are when he clearly knows the answer? Do you think John knew? Do you think you might have been able to puzzle it out had you been there?
7. Jesus is truly the Good Shepherd. He promises in this passage to guide us to springs of water of eternal life and to wipe away all of our tears. What about now? He promises in many places in Scripture to lead us as a shepherd, not just when we join

Him in heaven. Do you sense Him guiding you now and providing for you?

THE SEVEN TRUMPETS
Comparative Note

Chapters 8 through 11 of the Revelation deal with the Seven Trumpets. Depending on one's approach to interpreting the book, one can understand the trumpets in very different ways. As we consider Chapters 8-11, we need to answer the following questions:

- What do the Seven Trumpets represent in John's vision?
- When do these events occur relative to John's vision and the church age?

Historicist Approach

- The trumpets speak of a series of invasions against the Roman Empire (Vandals, Huns, Saracens, and Turks).
- The sixth trumpet signals the fall of Constantinople to the Turks in 1453.
- The little book (Chapter 10) represents the Bible being made available to the masses of Europe after the invention of the printing press.

Preterist Approach

- The first four trumpets correspond to disasters inflicted by the Romans on the Jews in the Jewish War (66-70AD).
- The fifth trumpet probably depicts the demonic spirits rendering the besieged Jews irrational and self-destructive.
- The sixth trumpet refers to the Roman armies, who destroyed Jerusalem and slaughtered or deported all Jews.

Futurist Approach

- Either literally or symbolically, the trumpets represent calamities that will be endured by the unrepentant inhabitants of earth during the coming seven-year Tribulation.

- These may be supernatural judgments direct from the hand of God or merely the disastrous effects of man's improper stewardship of the earth and his abuse of technology (for example, nuclear weapons).

Spiritual Approach

- Catastrophes reminiscent of the plagues of Egypt befall sinful humanity many times in history, demonstrating God's displeasure and, like the trumpet blasts, warning of worse things to come upon the unrepentant.
- The trumpets do not symbolize single and separate events, but they refer to calamities that may be seen any day of the year in any part of the globe. Thus the trumpets occur over the same period as the seals—during the church age.
- Sinful humanity typically absorbs these injuries with defiance, refusing to repent.

THE REVELATION
Chapter 8

The Seventh Seal. Revelation 8:1-2

- The Seal Broken.
  - The Lamb.
  - Silence.
- The Seal Dispatched.
  - Seven Angels.
  - Seven Trumpets.

The Prayers of the Saints. Revelation 8:3-5

- The Intermediary.
- Prayers of Saints.
  - Components of prayer.
    - Much incense.
    - Every prayer.
  - Implements of Prayer.
    - A golden censer.
    - The golden altar.
  - Destination of Prayer.
- Warning from Heaven.
  - Components of the warning.
    - Coals from the altar.
    - Cosmic disturbances.
  - Destination of the warning.

Preparation for the Trumpets. Revelation 8:6

The First Trumpet. Revelation 8:7

- Description.
  - Hail and fire.
  - Mixed with blood.

- Destination: Earth. See pages 151-152.
- Destruction.
  - A third of the earth burned.
  - A third of the trees burned.
  - A third of green grass burned.

The Second Trumpet. Revelation 8:8,9

- Description.
  - A great mountain.
  - Burning with fire.
- Destination: The Sea. See page 153.
- Destruction.
  - A third of the sea became blood.
  - A third of the sea-life died.
  - A third of the ships destroyed.

The Third Trumpet. Revelation 8:10,11

- Description.
  - A great star-Wormwood.
  - Burning like a torch.
- Destination: Rivers and Springs.   See page 154.
- Destruction.
  - A third of the waters became bitter.
  - A third of men died from the water.

The Fourth Trumpet. Revelation 8:12

- Description. See page 155.
  - A third of the sun darkened.
  - A third of the moon darkened.
  - A third of the stars darkened.
- Destruction.
  - Daytime shortened by one third.
  - Nighttime lengthened by one third.

The Three Woes Announced. Revelation 8:13

- The Eagle Flies.
- The Woes Announced.

Applications

1. The way one chooses to interpret the Revelation determines how the Seven Trumpets are understood. Do you see that if we adopt the Spiritual approach to interpretation the Trumpets happen throughout the Church Age just as the Seven Seals do?
2. In Revelation 8:1, John tells us that there is a period of silence in heaven for about half an hour. Do you remember as a kid waiting for your father to come home from work to deal with you for some offense? How long did a half an hour seem to you then? We would call this interval "the calm before the storm." Do you agree?
3. The prayers of the saints play a prominent role in this passage. Does prayer play a prominent role in your life? Do you think some of your prayers might be among those described here? Can you imagine your prayers going before God on His throne?
4. We understand the First Trumpet to represent various disasters which take place on the earth (that is, land) which afflict persecutors of the Church. Can you give some examples of land-based disasters that have targeted unbelievers over the centuries? Is it possible that believers also have perished or suffered in these events?
5. The Second Trumpet is understood to represent various sea-based disasters that afflict persecutors of the Church. Can you give some examples of such incidents that might have occurred over the centuries?
6. The Third Trumpet represents disasters that arise in the rivers and fresh waters of the earth. Floods certainly would fit into this category. The Big Thompson (Colorado) flash flood of 1976 killed seven Campus Crusade staff women and the Toccoa Falls (Georgia) dam break in 1977 killed many

73

Christians at the college. How do we explain these events as judgments of God against unbelievers?

7. We know that cosmic disturbances can create problems on earth. Sixty-one million years ago an asteroid collision with the earth resulted in the extinction of 1/2 to 2/3 of all species on earth. While this did not occur during the Church Age, it does illustrate the awesome destructive capability of these phenomena. Can you think of similar events that have affected mankind?

THE REVELATION
Chapter 9

The Fifth Trumpet. Revelation 9:1-11

- Description.
  - The Initiator Appears.
    - A star from heaven.
    - Fallen to the earth.
    - Given the key to the abyss. See page 156.
  - The Abyss Opened.
    - Smoke poured forth.
    - Fouling the sun and atmosphere.
  - The Destroying Locusts. See page 157.
    - Their appearance.
      - Like battle horses.
      - Crowns like gold.
      - Faces like humans.
      - Hair like women.
      - Teeth like lions.
      - Breastplates of iron.
      - Sound like chariots.
      - Tails like scorpions.
    - Their commander—Destroyer.
      - Abbadon—Hebrew.
      - Apollyon—Greek.
- Destination.
  - Their restrictions.
    - They could not harm.
      - The grass of the earth.
      - Any green plant-life.
      - Any tree on the earth.
    - They could not kill anyone.
  - Their instructions.
    - Torment unbelievers.
    - With great intensity.
    - For limited duration.

- Destruction.
  - Men will seek death, but not find it.
  - Men will long to die, but death will flee.

The First Woe. Revelation 9:12

Applications

1. Following the Spiritual approach to interpreting the Revelation, we believe the Fifth Trumpet informs us that God allows Satan throughout the Church Age to unleash demonic powers filling the world with their wicked influence and activities. Why would God allow this?
2. Can you think of any specific individuals or instances in history that we might conclude fit the conditions of the Fifth Trumpet? Explain how and why you think your example applies.
3. Even though we have never experienced locust plagues in this part of the world, we know that such events inflict total destruction on the land. Thus, the imagery John is given to convey the Fifth Trumpet warning is vivid. What in the imagery suggests that these events are temporary in duration?
4. John describes how when Satan unlocks the abyss, smoke billows forth obscuring the sun and polluting the atmosphere. Do you see that this is an apt description of the spiritual blindness that attends wicked men and women? It isn't an accident that wicked people often operate under cover of darkness.
5. Unfortunately, evil people often inflict injury and death on innocent victims. What can we say about the Holocaust of World War II or the genocide of Joseph Stalin, Pol Pot, or in Africa today? Would you think these incidents were satanic in origin? What about the impact of these events on believers?
6. I recall a movie recently having the name "Apollyon." Did you see it? It is interesting that Hollywood borrows names from Scripture, but you can take it to the bank that the story line was not from Scripture. What would be the outcome if some movie

producer decided to do a faithful portrayal of some of the events of the Revelation?

The Sixth Trumpet. Revelation 9:13-21

- Description. See page 158.
  - The Voice of God.
    - From the golden altar.
    - To the sixth angel.
    - "Release the four angels."
  - The Four Angels.
    - Bound at the Euphrates.
    - Prepared for an exact time.
  - Armies of Death.
    - Horses.
      - Heads like lions.
      - Mouths spewing plagues.
      - Tails like serpents.
    - Riders. Multicolored Breastplates.
- Destination—Mankind.
- Destruction.
  - One third of mankind killed.
  - Two thirds of mankind remaining.
    - They did not repent of:
      - Demon worship.
      - Idol worship.
    - They did not repent of:
      - Murder.
      - Sorcery.
      - Immorality.
      - Thefts.

Applications

1. We understand the Sixth Trumpet to represent war; not one particular war, but all wars—past, present, and future. We have

certainly seen our share of war just in our own lifetimes. Why do you suppose it is that we can't live in peace?

2. The Euphrates River was the eastern boundary of the promised land and of the Roman Empire. Thus, it served as a barrier to invaders from the east and symbolizes restraint upon the forces of evil. Do you think there are restraints in place on the forces of evil today? (No speculation.)

3. Much has been made of the number 200 million. Some think it refers to the actual number of troops in a specific army or armies—I have heard it used to describe the strength of the Chinese army. Do you understand that in all probability this is a symbolic number representing the implements of war throughout history?

4. John's description of the armies of death is certainly compelling. The horses and riders in his vision are terrifying to the imagination as well they should be. We have come a long way from the rocks of cavemen to Cobra helicopters and Warthog assault planes. Do you get the symbolism?

5. In verse 17 we have the repeated phrase, "fire and smoke and brimstone," and in verse 18 we are told that one third of mankind are killed by the three plagues—fire, smoke, and brimstone. Do you agree that this is an apt way to describe casualties of war? Remember the photo of the South Vietnamese girl running from a napalm explosion?

6. We are told that the survivors of these conflicts are essentially unfazed by the events they live through. That is pretty much the way it is. "The war to end all wars" was just one in a long series of wars—not the last war. Why is this? Why don't we learn from our experience?

THE REVELATION
Chapter 10

The Strong Angel. Revelation 10:1-3a

- His Origin: Heaven.
- His Appearance.
  - Clothed with a cloud.
  - A rainbow on his head.
  - His face like the sun.
  - His feet like pillars of fire.
- His Position.
  - His right foot on the sea.
  - His left foot on the land.

Dialog in Heaven. Revelation 10:3b-11

- The Strong Angel's Cry.
  - With a loud voice.
  - As a lion roaring.
- The Peals of Thunder.
- The Voice from Heaven: to John.
  - Seal up the message.
  - Don't record the message.
- The Strong Angel's Reply.
  - His right hand raised.
  - His oath proclaimed.
    - By God.
    - No delay.
- The Voice from Heaven: to John.
  - "Take the Book."
  - "From the angel."

[John takes the book from the angel.]

- The Strong Angel: to John.
  - "Eat the book."
  - "It will taste as sweet as honey."
  - "It will make your stomach bitter."

79

[John eats the book.
   It tasted as sweet as honey
   It made his stomach bitter]
- Voices from Heaven.
   - "You must prophecy again concerning:"
   - "Many peoples, nations, tongues, kings."

Applications

1. In Chapters 8 and 9, we have the first Six Trumpets following one right behind another. As we turn to Chapter 10, we are prepared to read of the Seventh Trumpet, but we find a pause in the action. We recall that we had the same pattern with the Seven Seals—Six Seals in quick succession, then a pause before the Seventh. Why do you suppose this is?

2. We don't know the identity of the "strong angel" in Chapter 10, but there are several hints that, while he is not Jesus, he is closely associated with Jesus. What are some of the associations between the strong angel and Jesus? Would you not agree that because of this association he speaks with more authority?

3. The position of the strong angel is of interest. John tells us that his right foot is on the sea and his left foot on the land. We take this to indicate that his message concerns the entire universe (all land and sea on the earth) and is to be heard by all. Does this seem to you a bit earth-centric? What does this say about intelligent life elsewhere in the universe?

4. John is ready to record the words spoken by the seven peals of thunder when he is told by God to seal up the words and not write them. What is going on here? We have no idea who/what the seven peals of thunder are, and apparently we must wait until God is ready to let us in on this to find out. Are you OK with this?

5. After this, the strong angel declares there shall be no further delay and that the mystery of God is finished. What does this mean? We understand it to signal that the final judgment of God's creation is imminent—it will come at once. Do you

agree that when God declares that it is finished, then everything will be known and it will be clear?

6. The little book mentioned in verses 2,8,9, and 10 clearly represents God's Word. John is instructed to eat the book. The disclosure that the book will be sweet to the taste but bitter to the stomach reminds us that the Gospel itself is glorious (it is Good News), but the proclamation of the Gospel is often accompanied by tribulation and persecution. Do you agree?

7. John is informed in verse 11 that he must prophecy again "concerning many peoples and nations and tongues and kings." Turn over to Chapter 17 and quickly scan the message of this chapter. Would you say that the prophecy of Revelation 10:11 is fulfilled in Chapter 17?

THE 1260 Days
Comparative Note

Chapters 11 through 13 of the Revelation deal with a time period of 1260 days. Depending on one's approach to interpreting the book, one can understand this period in very different ways. As we consider the material, we need to answer the following questions:

- What does the period of time represent in John's vision?
- When does the period of time occur relative to John's vision and the church age?

Historicist Approach

- The measuring of the temple represents the determining of the true remnant church in the papal church at the time of the Reformation.
- The 1260 days is actually 1260 years, the duration of the power of papal Rome. There is no general agreement regarding the actual time in history.
- The two witnesses represent the Waldenses, Albigenses, and others who resisted the papacy in the years before the Reformation. See page 159.
- The woman is the visible church persecuted by Imperial Rome prior to 313, and her male child is the true church within her, vindicated by the enthronement of Constantine.
- The two beasts represent different aspects of the papacy.

Preterist Approach

- The 1260 days is the period of the Jewish War, of Nero's persecution, or both.
- The two witnesses are either historic prophetic witnesses against the Jews prior to the downfall of Jerusalem or a representation of the civil and religious authority in Israel.

- The woman (Israel) gives birth to a child (the church), which flees Jerusalem (during the Jewish War) and is afterward persecuted by the devil.
- The first beast is Rome (or possibly Nero, or both) persecuting the church.
- The second beast is either the cult of the emperor, some zealous Roman procurator, or false prophets in Israel.

Futurist Approach

- The 1260 days refer either to a period of a literal three and one-half years at the end of the Tribulation or to two periods of that length totaling seven years.
- The two witnesses are two individual prophets yet to appear in Jerusalem—possibly Moses and Elijah or Enoch and Elijah. Alternatively, they may represent a larger witnessing body.
- The woman (faithful Israel) will be forced by persecution from the Antichrist to flee into the wilderness during the Tribulation.
- The first beast (The Antichrist) is a political world leader, and the second beast (The False Prophet) is his religious counterpart, who enforces universal worship of the first beast.

Spiritual Approach

- The 1260 days symbolize the entire church age. See page 160.
- The two witnesses are the church throughout the church age bearing testimony through its ministers and missionaries.
- The woman sustained in the wilderness is also the church.
- The first beast (The Antichrist) signifies political power that persecutes the church at any time in history and anywhere in the world.
- The second beast (The False Prophet) is false religion and especially that which utilizes political power to accomplish its ends.

THE REVELATION
Chapter 11

The Temple of God. Revelation 11:1,2

- The Assignment.
  - Characters.
    - "Someone" gave the assignment.
    - John carried out the assignment.
  - Equipment. A rod.
- The Instructions.
  - What to measure.
    - The Temple.
    - The Altar.
    - The worshipers.
  - What not to measure: The Outer Court.
    - It has been given to the nations.
    - It will be trampled under foot.

The Two Witnesses. Revelation 11:3-13

- Description of the Two Witnesses.
  - Their charge.
    - To be clothed in sackcloth.
    - To prophesy for 1260 days.
  - Their character.
    - Two olive trees.
    - Two lampstands.
  - Their protection: Fire from their mouths.
  - Their power.
    - To shut up the sky.
    - To harm the water.
    - To smite the earth.
- Death of the Two Witnesses.
  - Their opponent: The beast.
    - Battles them.
    - Overcomes them.

- Their bodies.
  - Left in the streets of Jerusalem.
  - Viewed by the masses of people.
  - Prevented from proper burial.
- Their impact.
  - Enemies celebrate.
    - Making merry.
    - Giving gifts.
  - Torment ended.
- Deliverance of the Two Witnesses.
  - Their resurrection.
    - Life from God.
    - Fear from enemies.
  - Their translation.
    - Voice from heaven.
    - Reaction from enemies.
- Destruction: A Great Earthquake.
  - Devastation.
    - One tenth of the city destroyed.
    - Seven thousand people killed.
  - Defiance.
    - Survivors were terrified.
    - They gave glory to God.

The Second Woe. Revelation 11:14

Applications

1. We understand the measuring of the Temple here to represent measuring or determining the magnitude of the true Church. Suppose Jesus appeared to you and told you to give Him a count of the true believers in your local church congregation. How would you go about answering His request?
2. The outer court here we understand to be a reference to the Court of the Gentiles—the place where those who weren't true Jews were permitted on the Temple Mount—and in the context of Chapter 11 we understand this to mean unbelievers. We all

know that churches throughout history have been attended by those who don't truly affirm faith in Jesus. Do you have such people at your church? What is to be done with them?

3. Some believe that the two witnesses described in Chapter 11 are two actual people—most usually Moses and Elijah (representing the Law and the Prophets)—who will literally stand in the streets of Jerusalem near the end of the age to testify against the wickedness of the world. Can you cite some arguments in favor of this position? Against?

4. According to the Spiritual approach of interpreting the Revelation, we understand the two witnesses to represent the church during the entire church age as it confronts the unbelieving world with the truth of the Gospel and God's provision for those who turn to Him. Cite some of the arguments for this position. Against.

5. The 1260 days are certainly problematic and we can't be dogmatic regardless of the view we hold on the meaning of this time period. Some hold that the 1260 days are actually years (Historicist and Spiritual interpreters), while some hold that a time period of three and a half years is meant (Preterist and Futurist interpreters). Where do you come down on this and why?

6. Regardless of whether you understand the two witnesses to be literal individuals or the Church, it will certainly be unsettling to the unbelieving world when God resurrects this (these) witnesses. The actual physical devastation that will accompany the deliverance of the resurrection of the witnesses will be terrifying. Don't you agree?

7. John tells us that those people who survive the great earthquake are terrified and give glory to God. What does this mean? Do these people actually become believers and accept God's provision for their former rebellion? All of them? Some of them? Any of them?

The Seventh Trumpet. Revelation 11:15-18

- Description.
  - Loud voices in heaven.
    - The kingdom of the world, has become
    - The kingdom of our Lord.
  - The Twenty-four Elders.
    - Fell on their faces.
    - Worshipped God.
      - "We give You thanks, O Lord…"
      - "You have begun to reign."
- Destruction.
  - God's wrath.
  - God's judgment. Of the Dead.
    - For believers: Rewards.
      - Your bond-servants the prophets.
      - The saints.
      - Those who fear Your name.
    - For unbelievers: Destruction.

The Sanctuary of God. Revelation 11:19

- Appearance.
  - The Temple was opened.
  - The ark of His covenant appeared.
- Atmosphere.
  - Flashes of lightening.
  - Peals of thunder.
  - An earthquake.
  - A great hailstorm.

Applications

1. I love the expression "the kingdom of the world has become the kingdom of our Lord," don't you? What does this really mean? We actually have prayed for this many times in the Lord's Prayer, "Thy Kingdom come, Thy will be done, on

earth as it is in heaven." It will be a time of great celebration when this actually comes to pass. Don't you agree?

2. The Seventh Trumpet actually signals the final judgment when God judges the human race according to their acceptance or rejection of Him. In John 5:24 the Apostle who wrote the Revelation writes, "... he who hears My word, and believes Him who sent me, has eternal life, and does not come into judgment, but has passed out of death into life." Does this apply to our passage here? How?

3. According to Indiana Jones and "Raiders of the Lost Ark" the Ark of the Covenant is lost in some huge government warehouse in the District of Columbia. But John tells us that the Ark will be seen in God's sanctuary in heaven. What is the significance of the Ark in John's vision?

THE REVELATION
Chapter 12

The Woman, the Child, and the Dragon. Revelation 12:1-6

- The Woman.
  - Her appearance.
    - Clothed with the sun.
    - Standing on the moon.
    - Crowned with twelve stars.
  - Her condition.
    - Pregnant with a child.
    - Crying out in labor.
  - Her destiny.
    - Fled to the wilderness.
    - Nourished by God.
    - For 1260 days.
- The Dragon.
  - His appearance.
    - A great red dragon.
    - Seven heads with diadems.
    - Ten horns.
  - His activity.
    - Swept away stars (angels).
    - Stood before the woman.
- The Child.
  - Would rule the nations.
  - Was caught up to God.

The War in Heaven. Revelation 12:7-12

- The Participants.
  - Archangel Michael.
  - Michael's angels.
  - Satan (the devil).
    - The serpent of old.
    - The deceiver of the world.

- Satan's angels.
- The Outcome.
  - Satan and his angels were overcome.
  - Satan and his angels were cast down.
- The Pronouncement. (By a Loud Voice.)
  - The salvation, power, and kingdom of God have come.
  - The authority of His Christ has come.
  - The accuser of our brethren has been thrown down.
- The Explanation.
  - By the blood of the Lamb.
  - By the testimony of the saints.
- The Conclusion.
  - Rejoice, O heaven!
  - Woe to the earth!
    - The devil is loose.
    - His Time is short.

The Dragon's Final Assault. Revelation 12:13-17

- The Woman's Plight.
  - Flies into the wilderness.
  - Nourished by the earth?
  - Helped by the earth.
- The Dragon's Revenge.
  - He targeted the woman.
  - He attacks her offspring.

Applications

1. Notice from our Book Chart of the Revelation on pages 23-25 that Chapter 12 marks the beginning of Part II of the book, which we have called The Cosmic Struggle. In other words, the focus of the action shifts now from earth to heaven. Do you see that the events of Chapter 12 do indeed suggest a cosmic conflict? How so?
2. The woman in Chapter 12 is thought to represent Israel (Futurists) or the believing remnant in Israel (Spiritualists).

Thus, the action, at least in the beginning of the chapter, takes place prior to the birth of the woman's child, Jesus. Do you agree? Do you think any other understanding makes sense?

3. The woman's child is clearly meant to represent Jesus; there is almost universal agreement on this point (Preterist, futurist, and spiritual). Historicists alone think the child represents "children of the church." Do you think that the fact that the child is to rule all the nations is a pretty good tip off? His being "caught up to God and His throne" is clearly speaking of the ascension of Jesus described in Acts 1. Do you agree?

4. Satan has been in the business of trying to derail God's plans for His creation since the day he was created. Throughout the Old Testament, he tried to get the Jews destroyed to thwart God's purposes. Do you see that this is so? In the temptation of Jesus in the wilderness, Satan tried to get Jesus to abandon God's plan. Read 1 Corinthians 10:13; do you see why it is so important for us to resist temptation?

5. The timing of the war in heaven described here is in dispute. If you are following the futurist approach to interpreting the book, you believe that the battle takes place at the midpoint of "The Tribulation" period, which is yet to come. Spiritual adherents, on the other hand, see this as happening at the death and resurrection of our Lord at which time Satan no longer has any accusation to make against believers. God's response to any such attempt is, "that has been taken care of by the death of My Son." How do you come down on this?

6. Since Satan's defeat when Jesus gave up His life on the cross, Satan has been limited in power to inflicting destruction and malice on planet earth. Looking back over the history of the last 2000 years, we must agree that he has been active. Toward what end is he working, seeing as how he has already been defeated?

7. Regardless of how you view the events of Chapter 12, the conclusion is infinitely better than any Saturday afternoon serial we watched at the movies when we were kids. The voice in heaven declares, "The salvation, and the power, and the

kingdom of our God and the authority of His Christ have come." Is that awesome, or what?

THE REVELATION
Chapter 13

[Satan is standing on the seashore.]

The Beast from the Sea (The Antichrist). Revelation 13:1-10

- The Beast. See page 161.
  - His appearance.
    - Ten horns, ten diadems.
    - Seven heads having blasphemous names.
      - One fatally wounded.
      - The wound healed.
    - Looked like a leopard.
    - Feet like a bear's.
    - Mouth like a lion's.
  - His authority.
    - Source: the dragon.
      - Power.
      - Throne.
      - Authority.
    - Duration: 42 months.
  - His activities.
    - Speech.
      - Spoke arrogant words.
      - Blasphemed God's person.
      - Blasphemed God's name.
      - Blasphemed God's people.
    - Actions.
      - Battled against the saints.
      - Overcame the saints.
    - Force. Exercised authority:
      - Over every tribe and people.
      - Over every tongue and nation.
- The World.
  - Unbelievers.
    - Those whose names are not in the book of life.

- - ▪ Worshiped the dragon.
    - ▪ Worshiped the beast.
  - - Believers.
    - ▪ Those whose names are recorded in the book.
    - ▪ Worshiped neither the beast nor the dragon.
- • The Warning. To believers.
  - - Listen.
  - - Persevere.
    - ▪ In captivity.
    - ▪ In battle.

The Beast from the Earth (The False Prophet). Revelation 13:11-18

- • The Beast. See page 162.
  - - His appearance.
    - ▪ Two horns like a lamb.
    - ▪ Spoke like a dragon.
  - - His authority.
    - ▪ Same as the Antichrist.
    - ▪ Depends on the Antichrist.
  - - His activities.
    - ▪ Performs great signs—fire from heaven.
    - ▪ Causes unbelievers to worship the Antichrist.
    - ▪ Deceives mankind because of the signs.
      - ▫ Forces men to create an image of the Antichrist.
      - ▫ Breaths breath into the image (brings it to life).
      - ▫ Threatens death for not worshiping the image.
    - ▪ Marks unbelievers with the name or number (of the Antichrist):
      - ▫ On his right hand.
      - ▫ On his forehead.
- • The World.
  - - Unbelievers.
    - ▪ Worshiped the Antichrist.
    - ▪ Worshiped the image of the beast.
    - ▪ Received the mark of the beast.

- Believers.
  - Did not worship the beast or the dragon.
  - Did not receive the mark of the beast.
- The Warning. To believers.
  - Understand.
  - Calculate.
    - The number of the man.
    - The number is 666.

Applications

1. At the beginning of the chapter, John tells us that he (the dragon) stood on the sand of the seashore. Do you see the symbolism of Satan standing by the sea summoning help in his campaign to wage war against the saints? Do you minimize the idea of Satan, or does this picture cause you concern?
2. From John's description, the beast from the sea which answers Satan's summons is horrific in appearance. We ought to know that Satan's accomplices are truly despicable in character. Read Daniel's vision in Daniel 7:1-8. Do you see the similarity of Daniel's vision and the beast of Revelation 13? How so?
3. We believe the beast of this chapter represents Satan's persecution of the Church and of believers through different nations and governments throughout the Church age. In this regard, the beast represents Satan's hand—carrying out his work of persecution through the centuries. The beast is called the Antichrist because he is in opposition to the things of Christ. What is your reaction to this representation?
4. It is difficult to probe too deeply into details. Some believe that the seven heads represent seven successive anti-Christian governments in history. They associate the head having the healed fatal wound with the Roman emperor Nero—who committed suicide, almost ending the empire—followed by Domitian who continued the persecution of Christians. Do you see why trying to associate specific events in history with symbolic events is similar to the problem of the Historicists?

5. The second beast is thought to represent false religions and philosophies of the world during the Church age, or anti-Christian wisdom—the devil's mind. Isn't it interesting that all of the false religions we know about have just a hint of similarity with Christianity (resemble the Lamb) that makes them somewhat plausible? Can you give some examples?

6. The second beast is sometimes called the False Prophet and as we see here, is a servant (dependent on) of the first beast. Isn't it interesting how governments and religion have often worked together in history to persecute the Church? Think of the Roman Catholic Church and the French Huguenots or the Church of England and the Puritans. What do you make of this? Coincidence?

7. In Revelation 5:1 we see that believers are sealed and we take this to be the sealing of the Holy Spirit (Ephesians 1:13)—the indwelling of the believer by the Holy Spirit of God. In Revelation 13 we have the sealing of the foreheads (the mind) or the hand (actions) of unbelievers by a mark—possibly the spirit of evil. Does this make sense?

8. We are not even going to try to fathom the mark "of a man, and his number is six hundred and sixty-six." I think the spirit of evil is close enough for this.

THE REVELATION
Chapter 14

The Lamb and His Flock. Revelation 14:1-5

- The Characters.
  - The Lamb.
  - The 144,000. Written on their foreheads:
    - The Lamb's name.
    - The Father's name.
- The Chorus.
  - Music. A voice from heaven.
    - Like the sound of many waters.
    - Like the sound of loud thunder.
    - Like the sound of many harpists.
  - Membership. The 144,000:
    - They are chaste.
    - They follow the Lamb.
    - They have been purchased.
    - They are the first fruits.
    - They are blameless.
  - Melody. A new song.

The Announcement of Judgment. Revelation 14:6-7

- The Messenger. An Angel.
  - Responsible for proclaiming the gospel.
  - To every nation and tribe and tongue and people.
- The Message.
  - Fear and glorify God.
  - Worship the Creator.
  - The hour of judgment has come.

The Announcement of Defeat. Revelation 14:8

- The Messenger. A Second Angel.

- The Message. Babylon the great:
  - Deceived unbelievers.
  - Will be destroyed.

Applications

1. Here again there seems to be a pause in the action, as John describes for us events which transpire in heaven. Can you imagine what it must have been like for John to eavesdrop on heaven? Suppose you had been in John's place. What might you have been thinking?
2. We concluded earlier that the number 144,000 represents all believers in all times and is to be taken symbolically rather than literally. Can you find support for this view here in the text of Chapter 14? What evidence suggests that this is a valid understanding of this mysterious number?
3. The first angel represents the proclamation of the gospel to mankind throughout the church age, always with the warning that judgment will follow at some future time. How do we wake up people who glibly pursue pleasure and comfort without concern for spiritual truth? Do you have family members or friends who fall into this category?
4. Babylon the great represents the seductiveness of the world. No one can doubt that the world offers some exciting and alluring temptations. But the days of the enticements of the world are numbered. Can you cite examples of people who have chased the seductions of the world to their own undoing or doom?
5. Notice the words John uses to describe the seduction of the world, "all the nations drink of the wine of the passion of her immorality." Do you think this aptly describes the allure of worldly temptations? Why or why not?
6. I have always thought that Egyptians must be somewhat put off by the narrative of the plagues in Egypt at the time of Moses. Similarly, I expect that knowledgeable people from the Middle East, especially Iraq, must be distressed by the biblical use of "Babylon" to characterize the immoral enticements of the

world. How should we handle this when sharing with individuals from this area of the world?

A Warning. Revelation 14:9-12

- The Messenger. A Third Angel.
- The Message.
  - To unbelievers. Those who worship the Beast.
    - You will drink of the wine of the wrath of God.
      - Mixed in full strength.
      - In the cup of His anger.
    - You will be tormented forever with fire and brimstone.
      - In the presence of angels.
      - In the presence of the Lamb.
    - You will have no rest day or night.
  - To believers. Persevere!
    - Those who keep the commands of God.
    - Those who keep their faith in Jesus.

A Blessing. Revelation 14:13

- The Messenger. A Voice from Heaven.
- The Message. Blessed are those who die in the Lord.
  - They may rest from their labors.
  - Their deeds follow with them.

Harvesting the Earth (The Elect). Revelation 14:14-16

- The Harvester. One Like a Son of Man.
  - Sitting on a white cloud.
  - Having a golden crown on His head.
  - Having a sharp sickle in His hand.
- The Messenger. Another Angel.
  - Crying with a loud voice.
  - Addressing the harvester.
- The Message: Reap!
  - The hour has come.

- The harvest is ripe.

Harvesting the Clusters (The Wicked). Revelation 14:17-20

- The Harvester. Another Angel.
  - Came from the temple.
  - Having a sharp sickle.
- The Messenger. Another Angel.
  - Came from the altar.
  - Having power over fire.
- The Message.
  - Gather the clusters.
  - The grapes are ripe.
- The Harvest.
  - The grapes are thrown:
    - Into the great winepress.
    - Of the wrath of God.
  - The winepress is trodden:
    - Outside the city.
    - Blood flows.
      - Up to horses' bridles.
      - For two hundred miles.

Applications

1. The announcement of the third angel is a warning of the nature of judgment awaiting all who reject God by persecuting His children. This is not a pretty picture; in fact, it is downright terrifying! What is necessary to escape this tribulation? Have you done what is necessary?
2. Verse 12 is intended to encourage all who face persecution and tribulation in this life by reassuring them that their faith will enable them to persevere. Has your faith enabled you to withstand persecution and trouble? Would you share some examples?
3. We understand verses 14-16 to represent the Lord Jesus gathering His chosen ones to Himself throughout the church

age. In John 4:34-36, Jesus tells the disciples that the fields are white for harvest, indicating that people are ready to respond to the gospel. Do you see the similarities between these two passages? Do you know for certain that you are one of Christ's elect (I John 5:13)?

4. There can be no doubt that verses 17-20 refer to the gathering of the wicked to face the judgment of God. It is interesting that the angel who issues the command to gather is described as having power over fire. What is this all about? Can you read between the lines?

5. The imagery of a winepress is appropriate to express the application of God's wrath to the wicked. Remember that the wicked are not destroyed, their lives are not snuffed out; they will endure God's wrath throughout eternity. Should this picture motivate us to try to win the souls of unsaved men and women?

6. In the light of the terrifying punishment that awaits all who reject God's offer of forgiveness and eternal life through His Son, what should we be doing to reach out to lost men (and women) around us? Can you suggest some ways we might more effectively engage other people in our discussions and study?

THE REVELATION
Chapter 15

The Sea of Glass. Revelation 15:1-4

- A Great and Marvelous Sign.
  - Seven angels.
  - Seven plagues.
    - Final expressions of:
    - The wrath of God.
- A Sea of Glass and Fire.
  - Victorious saints.
    - Over the beast.
    - Over his image.
    - Over his mark.
    - Over his number.
  - Worshipful saints. Holding harps of God.
- A Song of Celebration.
  - Composers.
    - Moses, the servant.
    - Jesus, the Son.
  - Contents.
    - The works of God: great and marvelous.
    - The ways of God: righteous and true.
    - The name of God: feared and glorified.
    - The worship of God: universal (all nations).
  - Catalyst: The revelation of God's righteous acts.

The Sanctuary of God. Revelation 15:5-8

- The Seven Angels.
  - Clothed in linen.
  - Clean and bright.
  - Girded with gold.
- One of the Four Living Creatures.
  - Gave the angels seven golden bowls.
  - Filled with the wrath of God.

- The Temple.
  - Was filled with smoke from the glory of God.
  - Was closed until the plagues were finished.

Applications

1. Once again, John gives us a glimpse of the scene in heaven prior to the releasing of the Seven Bowls of judgment. Notice this is similar to the interludes before the Seven Seals of Chapters 5 and 6 and before the Seven Trumpets of Chapters 8 and 9. The Sea of Glass and the chorus of praise remind us of the calm before the storm, don't you think?
2. Depending on which of the four approaches to interpreting the Revelation we are following, we will place the timing of this scene differently. Historicists place it at the end of domination of the Roman Catholic Church prior to the Reformation, Preterists place it prior to the destruction of Jerusalem in 70 AD. Futurists, of course, see this as happening at some future point in time, while Spiritualists believe these events take place contemporaneously with John's vision and before the Bowl judgments are released over the church age. What say you?
3. We believe the Sea of Glass mingled with fire which we first saw in Revelation 4:6, represents God's righteousness revealed in judgments upon the wicked—the fire obviously representing judgment. What is your reaction to this representation? The Sea of Glass communicates a sense of peace and serenity, but the fire adds a dimension of calamity. Would you agree?
4. It is certain that this picture is reassuring to believers in all times and places. Their victory over the forces of evil is complete, having achieved victory over the beast, over his image, over his mark, and over the number of his name—in other words, total victory. How would you say you were doing personally with respect to experiencing victory over the forces of evil in your life?
5. The scene in the Temple is similar to staging weapons before a battle. The seven angels are at the ready, attired for the mission they will soon undertake. They are given golden bowls of

wrath representing God's wrathful judgment on evil to be released throughout the church age. Do you get the impending sense of wrath to come? Does this picture inspire or terrify you? It should inspire.

6. John tells us that the temple was filled with smoke from the glory of God and from His power. Most people who reject God and His offer of salvation have a pretty low view of Him—most don't even acknowledge His existence. Do you suppose they might change their story if they could see God as He really is? Why or why not?

7. We are informed that no one is able to enter the temple until the seven plagues are completed. We take this to mean that once God has directed his judgments at an unbeliever, further intercession is fruitless. God's wrath, once initiated, will not be abated. Should this fact cause us to engage more energetically for our unbelieving friends and family? How so?

THE SEVEN BOWLS
Comparative Note

In Chapters 14 and 15, John describes the scene in heaven. Now he continues with his description of the judgments of God as He wages war against the dragon and his allies. In Chapter 16 we have the Seven Bowl judgments and as in previous sections of the book we can be sure that there are widely differing interpretations of these events. Again we will need to answer the following questions:

- What events do the Seven Bowls of wrath or plagues represent?
- When do these events occur relative to John's vision and the church age?

As we have noted the answers depend on which of the four major ways of interpreting the book one follows.

Historicist Approach

- The seven bowls find fulfillment in the judgment upon Babylon, which many adherents of this approach saw as the Roman Catholic Church (the papacy).
- According to this view, the events started with the French Revolution (1794-99) and the Napoleonic Wars (1799-1815) and will conclude in the future.

Preterist Approach

- The judgments of these bowls are primarily against Jerusalem, culminating in its fall in 70 AD. The fifth bowl may involve Rome, probably referring to the empire after Nero's suicide.
- An alternative view refers strictly to the judgment of God against the pagan Roman Empire and has nothing at all to do with Jerusalem.

Futurist Approach

- The bowls represent future, global judgments that are unparalleled in history in terms of their devastating effects.
- These judgments occur at the end of the Tribulation and culminate in World War III or the Battle of Armageddon.
- This battle will be the last to be fought by mankind and will end with the coming of Christ as He establishes His millennial kingdom.

Spiritual Approach

- The bowl judgments are related to the trumpet judgments in that the bowls may simply be a continuation of the trumpet judgments.
- The primary distinction between the trumpets and the bowls is that the trumpets are only partial and serve to warn the wicked while the bowls are complete and represent final judgment.
- The same event in history may serve as a trumpet judgment for one individual (a warning) and a bowl judgment (final judgment resulting in death) for another person.
- The bowl judgments, as the scrolls and the trumpets, recur repeatedly throughout the entire church age.

THE REVELATION
Chapter 16

The Bowls Summoned. Revelation 16:1

- The Voice.
- The Command.

The First Bowl. Revelation 16:2 [See page 151-2]

- The Bowl's Contents: Loathsome, Malignant Sores.
- The Bowl's Target: Men.
  - Who had the mark of the beast.
  - Who worshiped the beast's image.

The Second Bowl. Revelation 16:3   [See page 153]

- The Bowl's Contents: Blood.
- The Bowl's Target: The Sea.
  - The sea was polluted.
  - All sea life died.

The Third Bowl. Revelation 16:4-7 [See page 154]

- The Bowl's Contents: Blood.
- The Bowl's Target: Fresh Waters.
- The Angel's Comment
  - You are righteous, Lord.
  - You have judged, Lord.
    - They poured out the blood of saints.
    - You have given them blood to drink.
- The Altar's Reply: Your judgments are True and Righteous.

The Fourth Bowl. Revelation 16:8-9 [See page 155]

- The Bowl's Contents: Fierce Heat.

- The Bowl's Target: Men.
  - They blasphemed the name of God.
  - They did not repent to give God glory.

Applications

1. In Revelation 16:1, we hear a voice from the temple saying to the seven angels, "Go and pour out the seven bowls of the wrath of God into the earth." We aren't told who the voice belongs to, but we can tell that terrible things portend. The writer of Hebrews says, "It is a terrifying thing to fall into the hands of the living God. (Hebrews 10:31)." Wouldn't you agree?
2. We are told the First Bowl contains malignant sores, which we take to represent incurable diseases. While these maladies are specifically directed to unbelievers, we know that believers also suffer and die from such diseases. So what is going on here? What is the difference between an unbeliever dying from cancer and a believer dying from the same ailment?
3. The Second Bowl contains blood which is poured into the sea; we take this to represent all maritime disasters throughout the church age. We hear a lot these days about "Red Tides"—severe pollution, which kills everything in its wake. Does this sound a bit like wrath from the Second Bowl? Believers and unbelievers alike die in maritime disasters, right? Explain?
4. The Third Bowl also contains blood which contaminates fresh water sources and we believe this represents all calamities affecting water resources during the church age—droughts, shortages, pollution, etc. These calamities are God's revenge on those throughout history who have slain believers (martyrs). See Revelation 6:9-10 for background. Sometimes it appears like the wicked get away with murder. Do they?
5. Notice that the Second and Third Trumpets (Revelation 8:8-11) destroy a third of sea life and fresh water sources respectively, while the Second and Third Bowls completely destroy all sea life and all fresh water sources. This apparently happens at the end of the church age when God finally spills His wrath

completely. Isn't the parallelism interesting? Do you see the increasing intensity of the judgments?

6. The Fourth Bowl somehow affects the sun so that it accomplishes God's purposes by periodically afflicting the wicked—possibly drought, heat spells, and weather phenomena caused by sunspots, etc. Of course scientists would think it absurd that anyone could use the sun to accomplish his or her ends. What do you think?

The Fifth Bowl. Revelation 16:10-11

- The Bowl's Contents: Darkness.
- The Bowl's Target: The Throne of the Beast.
  - Men gnawed their tongues in pain.
  - Men blasphemed the God of heaven.
  - Men did not repent of their deeds.

The Sixth Bowl. Revelation 16:12-16

- The Bowl's Contents: Drought.
- The Bowl's Target: The Euphrates River.
- The Triumvirate's Response:
  - Mobilization of demons.
  - Gathering of kings.
- The Lord's Admonition [to Believers]: "I am Coming."
  - Stay awake, or
  - Suffer shame.

The Seventh Bowl. Revelation 16:17-21

- The Bowl's Contents: An Earthquake.
- The Bowl's Target: Babylon the Great.
  - Babylon was judged.
  - Cities were destroyed.
  - Islands disappeared.
  - Mountains vanished.
  - Hailstorms rained.

- Men railed.

Applications

1. The Fifth Bowl brings darkness and pain to "the throne of the beast." We take this to indicate that the centers of antichristian government are neutralized or nullified. Whenever any atheistic government falls, we can be assured that God is involved. I recall going twice to the former Soviet Union just after the curtain fell, and was amazed at the interest we found in Christianity and envy of the West. Do you believe God is involved in the rise and fall of government entities?
2. Evil people are often caught up in the schemes of evil governments. Organized crime is a huge problem in the U.S.S.R. today. Do you believe the former communist overlords were happy campers when the Soviet Union came unglued? Do you think government officials in the Peoples' Republic of China are happy about the openness that the Olympics brought to that country? Can you imagine them seeking forgiveness for past wrongs?
3. The Sixth Bowl ushers in Armageddon. The Red Dragon, the Beast, and the False Prophet respond by mobilizing their demonic forces throughout the church age and ultimately staging for the last great conflict which will signal the end of time as we know it. Frogs are a symbol of repulsive demonic activities. Do you get the symbolism?
4. The Seventh Bowl contains an earthquake which as we have seen with the Seals and the Trumpets is symbolic of Judgment Day. When God is finally ready to shut things down, all of the evil empires and organizations (Babylon) will be destroyed, and the earth (cities, islands, mountains) will be destroyed. And in those last remaining moments of time evil men will rail against God rather than seeking His forgiveness. Is God justified in His actions? (see 2 Peter 3:9)
5. Many have seen the similarities between the Old Testament plagues in Egypt and the Seals, Trumpets, and Bowls of Revelation. The plagues in Egypt were a systematic assault on

the polytheistic religious system of the Egyptians—through the plagues, God mocked every one of the Egyptian deities. The judgments of Revelation are a systematic assault on the godless government and social systems of our world and on the evil men and women who populate these entities. Do you get it?

THE GREAT BABYLON
Comparative Note

In Chapters 17-19, John describes Babylon and its judgment and fall, the coming of the Lamb, and Armageddon. These last chapters must be viewed through the lens of one of the four approaches to interpretation. Again we will need to answer the following questions:

- Who or what does Babylon represent—is it an actual city or does it represent a system?
- When does its judgment and fall occur relative to John's vision and the church age?

As we have noted the answers depend on which of the four major ways of interpreting the book one follows.

Historicist Approach

- The fall of Babylon the harlot is the overthrow of the papal system of religion and government. It will take place in the future (2015+).
- Chapters 17-19 present the different reactions of godly and ungodly people to the final vindication of true religion.
- The rider on the white horse represents the ongoing conquest of Christ through His word or through continuing judgment.

Preterist Approach

- Babylon is identified with either The Roman Empire or with the city of Jerusalem during the time before its destruction by the Romans.
- If Babylon is Rome, the events describe the downfall of the Roman Empire and especially the city of Rome, the harlot.
- If Babylon is Jerusalem, these visions depict the burning of the city by the Romans in 70 AD and the reactions of the wicked and the righteous.

Futurist Approach

- Babylon may represent the Roman Catholic Church or some great apostate religious entity working under the Antichrist in the end times (future).
- Alternatively, Babylon may be an actual city—either a restoration of ancient Babylon (presently deserted) or a revived Rome.
- Whichever, this great enemy of truth and righteousness will be destroyed at the end of the Tribulation; the wicked will mourn, the righteous rejoice.
- Jesus will return visibly to the earth riding a white horse (future).

Spiritual Approach

- Babylon represents the world system—anything that allures, tempts, seduces, and draws people away from God.
- Babylon's destruction at the end of the church age is depicted as it manifested itself in John's time as the city of Rome in 95 AD.
- The ultimate judgment upon the harlot comes through Christ at His Second Coming; He is the rider on the white horse.
- Alternatively, the rider may represent Christ's more gradual conquests over the world system through the spread of the gospel.

Babylon Described. Revelation 17:1-6

- Instructions.
  - From one of the seven angels.
  - For John to come and see.
- Description.
  - The harlot identified.
    - She sits on many waters.
    - She acted immorally with the kings of the earth.
    - She made people drunk with her immorality.
  - The harlot located.
    - She was found in the wilderness.
    - She was sitting on a scarlet beast.
      - Having seven heads and ten horns.
      - Filled with blasphemous names.
  - The harlot attired.
    - She was clothed in purple and scarlet.
    - She was adorned with gold, gems, and pearls.
    - She held in her hand a gold cup.
      - Full of abominations.
      - Full of her immorality.
    - She had written on her forehead.
      - Babylon the Great.
      - Mother of Harlots.
      - Mother of Abominations.
  - The harlot inebriated.
    - With the blood of saints.
    - With the blood of the gospel.
- Reaction. John Wondered.

Babylon Explained. Revelation 17:7-18

- Reassurance.
  - A question for John. Why wonder?

- An explanation of the mystery.
  - Regarding the woman.
  - Regarding the beast.
- Explanation.
  - The beast revealed.
    - His biography.
      - He was and is not.
      - He will come out of the abyss.
      - He will go to destruction.
    - His mystery.
      - Unbelievers see.
      - Unbelievers wonder.
    - His position. The eighth king
  - The kings arrayed.
    - Seven heads, seven kings.
      - Five have fallen.
      - One is living.
      - One will come for a time.
    - Ten horns, ten kings.
      - Have not received kingdoms.
      - Have received authority.
  - The battle disclosed.
    - The kings.
      - Adopt a common purpose ($\equiv$ God's purpose).
      - Give their kingdoms to the beast.
    - The Lamb.
      - Who is Lord of lords and King of kings.
      - Whose followers are called, chosen, faithful.
  - The outcome foretold.
    - The Lamb is victorious.
    - The ten kings and the beast.
      - Will hate the harlot.
      - Will isolate and strip the harlot.
      - Will eat the harlot's flesh.
      - Will burn the harlot.

- Other details portrayed.
    - Seven heads.
        - Where the harlot sits.
        - Represent seven mountains.
    - Waters.
        - Where the harlot sits.
        - Represent peoples, nations...
    - The woman.
        - Is the great city.
        - Reigns over kings.

Applications

1. In the Revelation, Babylon portrayed as a harlot, represents the seductiveness of the world—anything that allures, tempts, seduces, and draws people away from God. In this chapter, Babylon is described as "sitting on many waters and with whom the kings and people of the earth have committed immorality." It is not difficult to fathom that rulers and people throughout history have been enticed away from God by the things of the world. Would you agree?

2. John is told that the harlot is found in the wilderness sitting on a scarlet beast. How do we know that the beast is the Antichrist and not Satan? We understand that the harlot (worldly enticements) and the beast (antichristian nations and governments) work together to separate men from God. Describe some of the ways this alliance has played out in history.

3. Having seen the harlot with his own eyes, John is puzzled, and we are as well. He is given an explanation of what he has seen. He is told that the beast, earthly kings, the harlot, and unbelievers cooperate. The history of the beast informs John (and us) that he was, he comes out of the abyss, and he goes to destruction. This is simply another way of saying that evil nations and governments rise and fall. Had John seen this pattern repeated in history?

4. At John's writing, there had been five prominent empires: ancient Babylon (Genesis 11), Assyria, Babylonia, Medo-Persia, and Greece-Macedonia. Rome was in power when John committed the Revelation to paper. Do you see how this fits exactly with the description of the kings John was given? We don't think it fruitful to speculate about the king to come (some think it is the European Union, but that now stands at 27 countries and has outgrown the symbolism).

5. John is told that in pursuing godless policies, nations and governments are fulfilling God's purposes for his creation. How can this be? Consider the account of Israel's escape from Egypt in Exodus and Paul's review of that in Romans 9:17. Do you agree that God can use evil men and evil governments to accomplish his purposes? See the book of Habakkuk for the principle.

6. We see in this Chapter that Babylon is defeated by the Lamb and His followers. This, of course will happen finally at the Second Coming of Christ. But we can say it also happens whenever in history evil, godless regimes end. Think of Germany under Hitler; or Russia under Joseph Stalin; or Uganda under Idi Amin.

7. It should be encouraging to you to be able to look back over history (even recent history) and know that evil will be punished. We often say that the U.S. can't be the world's police force. Well, we don't have to be. The world has a just judge who knows every evil deed of every evil person or nation or government and He will ultimately square the books in a way that is perfectly just. Do you believe this?

THE REVELATION
Chapter 18

Babylon Is Fallen. Revelation 18:1-3

- The Messenger. An Angel.
  - Coming down from heaven.
  - Having great authority.
  - Illuminating the earth.
- The Verdict: Babylon is Fallen.
  - She has become a dwelling place of demons.
  - She has become a prison for unclean spirits.
  - She has become a prison for hateful birds.
- The Reason.
  - The nations have drunk her immorality.
  - The kings have committed immorality with her.
  - The merchants have profited from her immorality.

Babylon Is Judged. Revelation 18:4-20

- Believers Warned.
  - Not to participate in Babylon's sins.
  - To avoid contracting Babylon's plagues.
- Babylon's Sins.
  - Have piled as high as heaven.
  - Have been remembered by God.
- Babylon's Punishment.
  - Magnitude.
    - According to her deeds—double.
    - According to her poison—twice.
  - Extent.
    - To the degree that:
      - She glorified herself.
      - She lived sensuously.
    - To the same degree.
      - Give her torment.
      - Give her mourning.

- Reason.
  - She says in her heart.
    - I sit as a queen.
    - I am not a widow.
    - I will never see mourning.
  - God judges Babylon.
    - Her plagues will come.
    - Mourning and famine will come.
    - She will be burned with fire.
- Kings Amazed.
  - Their offense.
    - Committed acts of immorality.
    - Lived sensuously with her.
  - Their reaction.
    - Stood at a distance.
    - Feared her torment.
    - Saw her destruction.
  - Their lament: Woe, Woe!
    - Babylon, the great city...
    - Your judgment has come.
- Merchants Chagrined.
  - Their offense. Became rich from Babylon.
  - Their condition.
    - No one buys their cargoes.
      - Jewels.
      - Wood.
      - Spices.
      - Animals.
      - Slaves.
      - Cloths.
      - Products.
      - Grains.
      - Chariots.
      - Humans.
    - Men no longer find them.
  - Their customers.
    - Long for fruit that is gone.
    - Long for things that have passed:
      - Luxurious things.
      - Splendid things.

- Their reaction.
  - Stood at a distance.
  - Feared her torment.
- Their lament: Woe, Woe!
  - Babylon, who was adorned in splendor...
  - Your great wealth has been laid bare.
- Shipmasters, Sailors, Passengers Mourn.
  - Their occupation. Made their living by the sea.
  - Their reaction.
    - Stood at a distance.
    - Saw her destruction.
    - Threw dust on their heads.
  - Their lament: Woe, Woe!
    - Babylon, who had ships at sea...
    - Your great wealth has been laid waste.
- Believers Avenged.
  - Heaven commanded to rejoice.
    - Saints.
    - Apostles.
    - Prophets.
  - God has pronounced judgment.
    - For believers...
    - Against Babylon.

Babylon Is Eulogized. Revelation 18:21-24

- The Angel's Demonstration.
  - He threw a great millstone into the sea.
  - He likened the fall to Babylon.
    - It would be thrown down with violence.
    - It would be found no longer.
- Babylon's Future State.
  - Concerning creativity.
    - Music will cease.
    - Crafts will cease.
    - Industry will cease.

- Concerning joy.
  - Lamps will no longer shine.
  - Brides and bridegrooms will no longer be heard.
- Concerning guilt.
  - Nations were deceived by your sorcery.
  - Blood of prophets and saints was found in you.

Applications

1. In the Revelation, Babylon, portrayed as a harlot, represents the seductiveness of the world—anything that allures, tempts, seduces, and draws people away from God. Is this a problem that might have occurred in John's time, but which doesn't affect many today? Can you name some of the allures which draw people away from God in 2015?
2. In verse 4, believers are warned to "come out of" Babylon. What does this mean? Do you know believers who are flirting with worldly temptations? The apostle Paul wrote in 2 Timothy 2:3, "No soldier in active service entangles himself in the affairs of everyday life, so that he may please the one who enlisted him as a soldier." Do you see the connection between Paul's admonition and that of Revelation 18:4?
3. Babylon is punished for glorifying in herself and for living sensuously. We don't have to strain ourselves to figure out what living sensuously entails. What about glorifying ones' self? What is this all about? In Romans 12:3, Paul writes, "...I say to everyone among you not to think more highly of himself than he ought to think; but to think so as to have sound judgment, as God has allotted to each a measure of faith." Do you see the connection?
4. Revelation 18 continues by telling us that the kings of the world committed acts of immorality with Babylon. We can certainly think of many examples of kings and government officials who have offended in this way. Joseph Stalin, Idi Amin, Ferdinand Marcos, Rod Blagojevich and many, many others come to mind. Just heard that our own members of Congress voted to increase their office allowances by $90,000

each this year when the normal increase is only $30,000. Connection?

5. Merchants are guilty of growing rich from Babylon. Materialism and consumerism are certainly hallmarks of our times. I remember traveling in the former Soviet Union in 1989-90 and discovering that the people there just wanted to be like Americans who, in their view, had everything. It is sad that in our Western culture, we tend to equate quality of life with quantity of stuff. Do you see the problem here?

6. The illustration of the angel throwing a giant millstone into the ocean is certainly apt. All of us have at one time or another thrown a large rock into a lake or pond. There is usually a gigantic splash with froth and bubbles as the rock sinks to the bottom. Then nothing. Silence. It is too bad that more people in our time don't get the warning. How can we get them to think?

7. Do you see that at the end of the age, the world's attractions will vanish? Believers will find satisfaction in God. Unbelievers will be bereft of anything of beauty, meaning, or pleasure. Those who pursue pleasure end with nothingness; those who pursue God end with fullness and joy. Is there anything wrong with enjoying the world's pleasures? Would you censure us for enjoying our river cruise in France last summer?

8. The chapter closes by stating that the blood of prophets and saints and of all who have been slain on the earth are to be found in Babylon. Is this an overstatement? How is it possible that the blood of everyone slain on earth can be laid at the feet of involvement in the distractions of the world?

THE REVELATION
Chapter 19

The Marriage of the Lamb. Revelation 19:1-10

- The Great Multitude Crying.
  - Hallelujah! Hallelujah!
  - Salvation, glory, and power belong to the Lord.
    - Because He has judged the great harlot.
      - Who corrupted the earth.
      - Whose smoke rises eternally.
    - Because He has avenged His bond-servants.
- The Twenty-four Elders and Four Living Creatures Saying.
  - Hallelujah! Amen!
  - Prostrate in worship.
- A Voice from the Throne Saying.
  - Give praise to God.
  - All of His bond-servants.
    - All who fear Him.
    - Great and small.
- The Great Multitude Saying.
  - Hallelujah! The Lord reigns.
  - Let us rejoice and be glad.
    - The Lamb's marriage has come.
    - The Lamb's bride has made herself ready.
      - She is clothed in fine linen.
      - She is bright and clean.
- The Voice from the Throne Saying.
  - Write: "Blessed are those who are invited."
  - Words: "These are the true words of God."
- John. Falling to Worship.
- The Voice from the Throne Saying.
  - "Don't worship me; I'm a fellow servant."
  - "Do worship God."
    - "The testimony of Jesus..."
    - "Is the spirit of prophecy."

The Coming of the King. Revelation 19:11-16

- His Person.
  - His character.
    - He is called faithful and true.
    - He judges in righteousness.
    - He wages war in righteousness.
  - His appearance.
    - His eyes are flames of fire.
    - His crown is many diadems.
    - His name (written).
      - Is written on Him.
      - No one knows it.
    - His robe. Dipped in blood.
      - KING OF KINGS.
      - LORD OF LORDS.
    - His name (spoken). The Word of God
    - His mouth. A sword.
  - His actions.
    - He smites the nations.
    - He rules the nations with a rod of iron.
    - He treads the winepress of God.
- His Army.
  - Clothed in linen.
    - Fine linen.
    - White and clean.
  - Follows on white horses.

Armageddon Announced. Revelation 19:17-18

- The Announcer. An Angel.
  - Standing in the sun.
  - Crying in a loud voice.
- The Call.
  - Come, assemble for...
  - The great supper of God.

- The Called. Birds of Midheaven.
  - Eat the flesh of...
    - Kings.
    - Commanders.
    - Mighty men.
  - Eat the flesh of horses.
  - Eat the flesh of all men.
    - Free men and slaves.
    - Great men and small.

Armageddon Completed. Revelation 19:19-21

- The Combatants.
  - The Lamb and His army.
  - The beast (and the false prophet).
    - The kings of the earth.
    - With all their armies.
- The Outcome.
  - The beast and the false prophet.
    - Were taken alive and thrown...
    - Into the lake of fire.
  - The rest were killed by the Lamb's sword.
  - The birds were filled with flesh.

Applications

1. John reports that there is great rejoicing and praise in heaven at the destruction of Babylon, the great harlot. We understand Babylon to be the world system—anything that would allure men and women away from God. Given that there is so much evil in the world, it probably might be a good thing to wipe it all out and start over, wouldn't you think?
2. We can sense the great excitement in heaven at the impending marriage of the Lamb. We are told that the bride (the Church) has readied herself arrayed in fine linen and washed clean and bright which speaks of moral purity. What about you? As part of the bride—the Church—are you concerned for your moral

purity? Are you trusting Jesus to protect you from the evil of the world?

3. In Revelation 19:10 we are told that "the testimony of Jesus is the spirit of prophecy. What do you suppose this means? Do you think it might mean that the spirit and content of all prophecy—of the entire Bible—is the story of Jesus; His work and words while He was on earth? Do you understand that the entire Bible is about Jesus? How so?

4. We are informed that the character of Jesus is faithful and true, that He judges and wages war in righteousness. Can you see the contrast between Jesus and the forces of evil aligned against Him? Aren't you attracted by the character of Jesus? Even if you didn't know that much about Him wouldn't you rather serve Him than the forces of evil?

5. Jesus is described to us in detail in Chapter 1. Go back and review that description. Does the description given here match that of Chapter 1, or does it complement the earlier version? Even if you hadn't read the earlier version, don't you think you would have been able to identify Him from the description given here? John describes Jesus in John 1:1 as the Word of God—that should help. Right?

6. John doesn't spend much time describing the army of Jesus other than to say that it is clean and clothed in fine linen and is following Him? John heard Jesus command Peter in John 21 to "Follow Me." When you think about it, our instructions as believers are pretty simple—we're just to follow Him. How does one do this?

7. When we are told in verse 20 that the beast (Antichrist) and the false prophet are thrown into the lake of fire, we should breathe a tremendous sigh of relief. Antichristian governments and false religions have together claimed hundreds of millions of lives and have made men's lives miserable throughout history. Can you identify some of the deeds of these two evil figures in your own lifetime?

8. After the beast and the false prophet are dispatched, John tells us that "the rest" are killed by the Lamb. In other words, Jesus fights our battles for us. Does this mean that we can simply sit

back and let Jesus take care of everything for us? Or does He expect for us to roll up our sleeves and jump into the fray? What does this mean for you—I have a pretty good idea of what He has in mind for me?

9. Armageddon is complete and final. Only Satan is left to be dealt with and that is done in Chapter 20. Do you get the sense of climax that is being communicated here? We may be in heaven cheering when the end comes or we may be on earth gutting it out; regardless, it will be a time for great rejoicing and for honoring the One who brought it about—don't you think?

THE MILLENNIUM
Comparative Note

One of the most perplexing concepts in Scripture is Revelation 20—specifically those verses dealing with the 1,000 year reign of the saints, commonly called the Millennium. Unfortunately, the four approaches to interpreting Revelation can't help us in understanding the final three chapters of the book, just as they don't apply to the first three. This is because none of the four approaches uniformly agrees with a single interpretation of Revelation 20. There are three approaches or ways of understanding the Millennium: Premillennialism, Amillennialism, and Postmillennialism.

Premillennial Approach

- The binding of Satan is still in the future. It will take place when Christ returns.
- The 1,000 years is a literal period during which Christ will reign on earth from Jerusalem with His people.
- The loosing of Satan will bring the Millennium to its climax, followed by the resurrection and judgment of the wicked at the Great White Throne.
- A new heaven and a new earth will be created after the Millennium, that is, 1,000 years after Christ's Second Coming.

Amillennial Approach

- The binding of Satan represents the victory of Christ over the powers of darkness accomplished at the cross.
- The 1,000 years is symbolic of a long, indeterminate period corresponding to the church age (from 95AD until Christ's Second coming).
- Satan will be released briefly to do his work and to persecute the church at the end of the church age.
- The fire coming from heaven and consuming the wicked is symbolic of Christ's Second Coming.

- A general resurrection and judgment of the evil and the good will occur at Christ's coming, followed by the creation of a new heaven and a new earth.

Postmillennial Approach

- Some interpret Chapter 20 similarly to the Premillennialists but with an added note of optimism about the success of the gospel in the present age.
- Others see the binding of Satan to represent a future point in time when the successful preaching of the gospel will have reduced Satan's effect to nothing.
- The 1,000 years may or may not be a literal duration, but speaks of a future glorious age, prior to the Second Coming when the influence of the gospel will be universal.
- A final attempt by the loosed Satan at the end of the age will amount to nothing.
- A general resurrection and judgment will occur at the coming of Christ.

THE REVELATION
Chapter 20

The Binding of Satan. Revelation 20:1-3

- The Angel.
  - Came down from heaven.
  - Held in his hand:
    - The key to the abyss.
    - A great chain.
- The Dragon.
  - His identity.
    - The serpent of old.
    - The devil, Satan.
  - His destiny. Bound for 1,000 years.
    - Thrown into the sealed abyss.
    - Prevented from deceiving nations.
    - To be released for a short time.

The Reign of the Saints. Revelation 20:4-6

- Reigning for 1,000 Years.
  - Who. **Souls** of Believers.
    - Those who had been beheaded.
    - Those who had not:
      - Worshiped the beast.
      - Received his mark.
  - What.
    - They came to life.
    - They reign with Christ.
- The First Resurrection.
  - Unbelievers for judgment.
  - Believers for eternal life.
    - To be blessed and holy.
    - To escape the second death.
    - To be priests of God.
    - To reign with Christ.

The Final Conflict. Revelation 20:7-10

- Satan Released.
  - To deceive the nations. Gog and Magog.
  - To mobilize his forces. Innumerable.
- Armies Engaged.
  - Surrounding the saints.
    - On the great plain.
    - Around the beloved city.
  - Devoured by fire.
- Satan Confined.
  - Consigned to the lake of fire.
    - Satan, the dragon.
    - The beast, the Antichrist.
    - The False Prophet.
  - Tormented forever and ever.

The Great White Throne. Revelation 20:11-15

- The Judge. God.
  - Earth and heaven fled from Him.
  - Earth and heaven were destroyed.
- The Judgment.
  - The judged.
    - Great and small before the throne.
    - The sea gave up its dead.
    - Death and Hades gave up their dead.
  - The standards.
    - The *Book of Life*.
    - The *Book(s) of Deeds*.
  - The sentences.
    - Death and Hades relegated to the lake of fire.
    - Unbelievers consigned to the lake of fire.

Applications

1. Following the Amillennial approach we understand the 1,000 years of Christ's reign to be symbolic of a long, indeterminate period corresponding to the church age (from 95AD until Christ's Second Coming); the Premillennial approach holds that the 1,000 years is a literal period yet to come during which Christ will reign on earth from Jerusalem with His people. What do you think?

2. According to Revelation 20 and other passages, when believers die during the church age, their souls go immediately to heaven to join Christ and reign with Him there. Paul writes in 2 Corinthians 5:8, "I ... prefer rather to be absent from the body and to be at home with the Lord." Of course their bodies remain in the grave (or wherever) until the resurrection. Is this comforting to you?

3. When unbelievers die during the church age, their souls go immediately to Hades—the abode of the unsaved between death and the Judgment. In the Parable of the Rich Man and Lazarus, Jesus speaks of the rich man dying and going to Hades (Luke 16:19-31). Hades is not a joke—regardless of what some may think. Should this motivate us to be concerned for the unsaved?

4. In Revelation 20 we are informed that Satan, the Beast (antichristian nations and governments) and the False Prophet (antichristian religion and philosophy) will be cast into the lake of fire to be punished eternally for their deception resulting in men and women being drawn away from the Father. [In Matthew 11:23 and Luke 10:15, Jesus warns a city that it will be cast into Hades.] What a relief it will be when these three are permanently removed from God's new creation. Do you agree?

5. When Jesus comes again at His Second Coming, the bodies and souls of all men, women, and children will be reunited—believers and unbelievers. Paul writes in 1 Thessalonians 4:16-17, "For the Lord Himself will descend from heaven with a shout, with the voice of the archangel and with the trumpet of

God, and the dead in Christ will rise first. Then we who are alive and remain will be caught up together with them in the clouds to meet the Lord in the air, and so we shall always be with the Lord." If you are a believer, this will be a great day; don't you agree?

6. If you have placed your faith in Christ, your name is written in the Lamb's *Book of Life* and you are not judged, thereby escaping the so-called second death. Jesus said in John 5:24, "Truly, truly, I say to you, he who hears My word, and believes Him who sent Me, has eternal life, and does not come into judgment, but has passed out of death into life." WOW! What a promise. Is your name in the book?

7. If one's name is not in the *Book of Life*, the *Book of Deeds* is opened and he or she is judged on the basis of their deeds. For those who are counting on getting a pass because they are "not as bad as their neighbor" or they "try to keep the Ten Commandments," God doesn't grade on the curve. Galatians 3:10 lays out the standard, "For as many as are of the works of the Law are under a curse; for it is written, 'CURSED IS EVERYONE WHO DOES NOT ABIDE BY ALL THINGS WRITTEN IN THE BOOK OF THE LAW, TO PERFORM THEM [emphasis in the Scripture].'" You don't want to be here, do you?

8. I have a university professor friend who relates that he was sharing the plan of salvation with a colleague over lunch one day. When he finished, his friend replied, "If I really believed that those in life who don't accept Christ go to a godless eternity, I would stop everything I'm doing and spend the rest of my life trying to persuade everyone." Do you understand what is at stake for yourself; for others?

The New Heaven and the New Earth. Revelation 21:1-8

- God's Creation.
  - The universe.
    - A new heaven and earth.
    - The old heaven and earth.
      - Has passed away.
      - The sea is gone.
  - The Holy City.
    - A new Jerusalem from heaven.
    - As a bride adorned for her husband.
  - God's involvement.
    - His tabernacle will be among men.
    - He shall dwell among them.
    - He Himself shall be among them.
- God's Work.
  - On behalf of believers.
    - Who He is.
      - He makes all things new.
      - He is the Alpha and Omega.
    - What He does.
      - He wipes away every tear.
      - He does away with death.
      - He eliminates pain and suffering.
      - He freely gives the water of life.
      - He gives an inheritance to believers.
      - He is the Father of His children.
  - On behalf of unbelievers.
    - Who they are.
      - Cowardly...
      - Liars.
    - What they receive.
      - The lake of fire.
      - The second death.

The New Jerusalem. Revelation 21:9-27

- The Bride Revealed.
  - By one of the seven angels.
    - Who held the bowls...
    - Containing the plagues.
  - From a very high mountain.
  - Coming down from heaven.
- The Bride Described.
  - Her radiance.
    - Glory.
    - Brilliance.
  - Her construction.
    - The city. Pure gold.
    - Walls.
      - Great and high. Seventy-two yards.
      - Twelve gates.
      - Twelve foundation stones.
    - Gates.
      - Twelve Angels. Each bearing the name of a tribe.
      - Twelve Pearls. Each gate a single pearl.
      - Never close. Ornamental only.
    - Foundation stones.
      - Each bearing the name of an apostle.
      - Each adorned with a precious stone.
    - Streets.
      - Pure gold like...
      - Transparent glass.
    - Her temple. None, not needed.
      - The Lord God.
      - The Lamb.
  - Her measurements.
    - By the angel. With a gold measuring rod.
    - Her dimensions.
      - Length. 1,500 miles.
      - Width. 1,500 miles.
      - Height. 1,500 miles.

- Her illumination.
  - Daytime. Always.
  - Nighttime. Never.
- Her visitors.
  - Kings of the earth.
  - The glory of nations.
- Her inhabitants.
  - Those whose name is written in the **Book of Life**.
  - Others shall never enter the city.

Applications

1. Man has always marveled at the creation. Many think it has always existed—they don't want to attribute it to a Creator. Most acknowledge that it had a beginning—and thus a Beginner. John tells us here that God destroys (or renews) the original creation to begin again. What do you think? Is this believable? Possible? Likely? What does it say about the creative power of the God we worship?

2. John tells us that in the new Jerusalem, God will live with His people and He will dwell among them. During the Exodus, God's presence was manifested to the Israelites in the cloud by day and the column of fire by night. But in heaven He will be revealed in all of His glory for all to see. That will be special. And it will take some getting used to, don't you think?

3. We often speculate about what heaven will be like. Here John tells us—there will be no tears, no death, no pain or suffering, everyone will have an inheritance, and God will be a Father to His children. How does that sound to you? I can't imagine that anyone would want to miss out on that, can you? Have you made your reservation?

4. Many people today refuse to believe in God because of the pain and suffering they observe in the world. Their reasoning goes like this, "If God were all powerful and all good, He would not allow pain and suffering in His creation. Since pain and suffering are facts of our existence, God is either not all powerful or not all good or He is neither. Regardless, I'm not

interested." What do we say to such people in the light of Revelation?

5. To view Jerusalem today, the Mount of Olives is easily the best vantage point—the city is spectacular from there at any time of day or night. John relates that he was taken to the top of a high mountain to view the new Jerusalem. The similarity is striking. I have always been blown away by all of the parallels in Scripture—this being to me one of the evidences of its divine origin. Do you agree?

6. John's description of the physical dimensions and features of the new Jerusalem should evoke awe from a reasonable person. Think of the most magnificent travel brochure you have ever seen. Then multiply that by a thousand. A city of gold. Streets of gold. A 1,500 mile cube. Is this not awesome? One could never tire of living in such a place, and when you think that God and Jesus will both be there, it will be exciting. What do you think?

7. John tells us that there is no night in heaven—it is always daytime. And there is no need for any source of light—not the sun, nor the moon. "For the glory of God has illumined it, and its lamp is the Lamb." Darkness is always symbolic of evil; men usually accomplish their evil purposes under cover of darkness. Think of living in a place which is always light. This will be different. But for the better?

8. We are told that the inhabitants of the new Jerusalem will be God, Jesus, the angels, the twenty-four elders, the four living creatures, the kings of the earth (only good kings need apply), and us—you and me. There will be no evil person or being. No evil is allowed. I could get accustomed to such a place, couldn't you?

9. The term "the bride" is used in Scripture to refer to the church. In Chapter 21, we are told that the New Jerusalem is the Bride of the Lamb; thus we conclude that the new city, is simply the residence of the bride—the church. This should make the images of the new Jerusalem presented here all the more special to you. The New Jerusalem is not just a geographical place, it is a family—the family of God. Get it?

137

THE REVELATION
Chapter 22

The New Jerusalem. Revelation 22:1-5

- The River of the New Jerusalem.
  - River of the water of life.
  - Coming from the throne.
    - Of God.
    - Of the Lamb.
- The Tree of the New Jerusalem.
  - Its location.
    - In the middle of the street.
    - On both sides of the river.
  - Its bounty.
    - Twelve kinds of fruit (one per month).
    - Leaves for the healing of the nations.
- The God of the New Jerusalem.
  - The throne of God and Jesus will be there.
  - The bond-servants of God and Jesus:
    - Shall serve God.
    - Shall see God's face.
    - Shall bear Christ's name.
- The Character of the New Jerusalem.
  - The curse is removed.
  - There shall be no light.
  - The Lord God shall illuminate it.
    - No need of a lamp.
    - No need of the sun.
  - God's saints shall reign.

The Authority of Revelation. Revelation 22:6-7

- The Character of the Book. Faithful and True.
- The Source and Purpose of the Book.
  - The Source. The Lord God.

- The Purpose.
  - To show God's bond servants...
  - Things which will shortly take place.
- The Promise of the Book.
  - Its author is coming again soon.
  - Its reader is blessed for obedience.

The Authority of the Author. Revelation 22:8-9

- John's Involvement.
  - He heard and saw these things.
  - He fell down to worship the angel.
- The Angel's Response.
  - Don't worship me.
  - I'm a fellow servant.
    - Of yours.
    - Of the prophets.
    - Of obedient saints.
  - Do worship God.

A Serious Warning. Revelation 22:10-15

- From an Angel.
  - Regarding the book.
    - Don't seal up the book...
    - For the time is near.
  - Regarding men.
    - Unbelievers.
      - Let the one who does wrong continue.
      - Let the one who is filthy continue.
    - Believers.
      - Let the one who is righteous continue.
      - Let the one who is holy continue.
- From Jesus.
  - Who I am.
    - I am coming quickly.
      - My reward is with Me.

        ▫ To reward men for their deeds.
    ▪ I am the Alpha and the Omega.
        ▫ The first and the last.
        ▫ The beginning and the end.
- What I will do.
    ▪ For those who wash their robes—blessing.
        ▫ Access to the tree of life.
        ▫ Entry to the gates of the city.
    ▪ For all others—denial.
        ▫ Dogs, sorcerers, immoral people.
        ▫ Murderers and idolaters.
        ▫ Those who love and practice lying.

The Authority of Jesus. Revelation 22:16

- I Have Sent My Angel.
    - To testify these things.
    - For the churches.
- I Am:
    - The root and offspring of David.
    - The bright and morning star.

An Invitation. Revelation 22:17

- From the Spirit and the Bride.
- Come and Drink Freely.
    - For the one who is thirsty.
    - For the one who desires the water of life.

A Second Warning. Revelation 22:18-19

- Jesus' Testimony Concerning the Revelation…
- To Those Who Hear the Words of This Book.
    - If you add to the words, God will add to you the plagues.
    - If you take away from the words, God shall take away:
        ▪ Your part of the tree of life.

- Your part of the holy city.

John's Response. Revelation 22:20

- I Heard These Things from Jesus.
- Amen, Come, Lord Jesus.

John's Benediction. Revelation 22:21

Applications

1. I've been in some really picturesque villages in Germany and France with streams flowing through them. The New Jerusalem will be infinitely more beautiful than anything we have ever seen. Sounds like a good place to settle down, don't you think?
2. In Exodus 33:20 we are told by God that, "You cannot see My face, for no man can see My face and live!" Yet here in the closing verses of the Bible, we read that in the New Jerusalem we will see God's face. What a remarkable privilege! Are you ready?
3. John restates the purpose of Revelation—to show God's bond-servants things that will shortly take place. Having come to the end of our study of this enigmatic book, do you feel like you have a good grasp of at least the broad sweep of the book? Could you give someone a 50 cent tour of the book? Could you lead someone through your notes?
4. We often get down on ourselves for making the same mistakes over and over again. Here in the space of a few chapters, John falls on his face twice to worship an angel and is admonished. Notice there are no lightening bolts. Do you think God forgave him? Do you think God forgives you when you repeat the same offenses?
5. In Daniel 12:4, Daniel is instructed to seal up the book, that is, to keep secret a vision which he had had concerning the last days. Here John is told not to seal up the book "for the days are near." Someone in Daniel's day might have been forgiven for not wondering about the end times. We have no excuses for not

probing to understand God's end game. What do you think? Was it worth it to slog through this difficult book? In what respect?

6. In this chapter Jesus promises us that we will have access to the tree of life and will be granted entry to the city. The world will be gone then; there will only be two destinations—the New Jerusalem and the lake of fire. Not a very difficult choice is it? Are there any folks you might want to hi-jack so that they come along with us to the New Jerusalem? What can you do to help them change their destination?

7. There is a pretty severe warning to those who would either add or subtract from God's word—Genesis to Revelation. This applies to the "prophet" Mohammed and to the "prophet" Joseph Smith, and all others who have attempted to add "a human touch" to the divine book. Does this mean we can simply ignore these texts? Or is it incumbent upon us to study them? For what purpose and to what end?

APPENDIX

REVELATION ILLUSTRATIONS

THE REVELATION
Interpretation Approaches: In Vogue

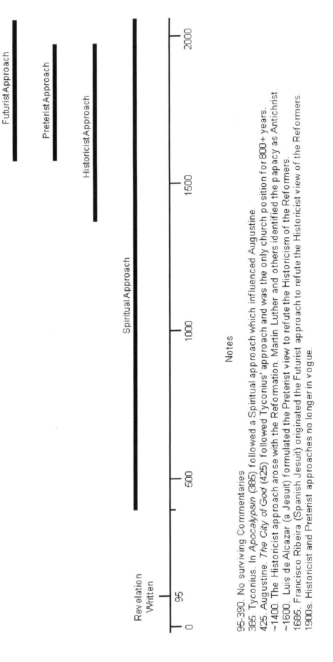

Futurist Approach

Preterist Approach

Historicist Approach

Spiritual Approach

Revelation
Written

| 0 | 95 | 500 | 1000 | 1500 | 2000 |

Notes

95-390. No surviving Commentaries

385. Tyconius. In *Apocalypsin* (385) followed a Spiritual approach which influenced Augustine.

425. Augustine. *The City of God* (425) followed Tyconius' approach and was the only church position for 800+ years.

~1400. The Historicist approach arose with the Reformation. Martin Luther and others identified the papacy as Antichrist.

~1600. Luis de Alcazar (a Jesuit) formulated the Preterist view to refute the Historicism of the Reformers.

1685. Francisco Ribeira (Spanish Jesuit) originated the Futurist approach to refute the Historicist view of the Reformers.

1900s. Historicist and Preterist approaches no longer in vogue.

144

REVELATION ILLUSTRATIONS
Examples of Principle 8

- Interpreting Revelation with Revelation
  - Revelation 20:1-3
  - Revelation 12:9

- Interpreting Revelation with the New Testament
  - Revelation 19:11-13
  - John 1:1

- Interpreting Revelation with the Old Testament
  - Revelation 13:1-10. Beast with:
    - Ten horns, seven heads
    - Leopard
    - Bear
    - Lion
    [What is this? The Antichrist, governments which persecute believers.]
  - Daniel 7:2-8. Four beasts:
    - Lion. Babylon
    - Bear. Medo-Persia
    - Leopard. Greece
    - Ten-horned beast. Rome
    [What is this? Kingdoms which persecuted believers.]

Note. Page 18 in the Study Guide.

REVELATION ILLUSTRATIONS
The Meta Story of History

In Heaven.

- God and His Host.
  - God reigns.
  - Angels serve.
- Satan and his Demons.
  - Satan rebels.
  - Demons follow.

On Earth.

- The Old Dispensation. (BC)
  - God prepares a people.
  - God prepares the world. Galatians 4:4
  - God prepares His word.
- The New Dispensation. (AD)
  - The Savior comes.
  - The Church is established.

Note. Introduction to Overview on page 21 of the Study Guide.

The Seven Churches of Revelation

	Ephesus	Smyrna	Pergamum	Thyatira	Sardis	Philadelphia	Laodicea
Distinctives Of City	Beautiful City Temple of Diana	1st City of Asia Temple-Emperor	Temple-Caesar Library #2 in world	Trade & Guilds Temple of Sambethe	Capital of Lydia Large Jewish population	"Little Athens" Founded by King Eumenes	Great & Wealthy Commerce Water & Meds
Distinctives Of Church	Est. by Paul Led by John	Est. by Paul Led by Polycarp	Unknown	Founded by Lydia?	Unknown	Unknown	Unknown
Bishop	John	Polycarp	Unknown	Unknown	Unknown	Unknown	Unknown
Self-Designation	Holds 7 stars Walks among lampstands	First & Last Come to Life	Sharp two-Edged sword	Eyes like flame Feet like bronze	He who has; Seven spirits Seven stars	Holy & True Keys of David	The Amen Faithful witness Beg. Creation
Commendation	Deeds & works Test apostles	Tribulation Poverty Opposition	Held My Name Did not deny Me	Love & service Increasing deeds	Your deeds & reputation	Your deeds Kept My word Didn't deny Me	None!
Condemnation	Lost first love	None!	False Doctrine	Conformity	Immorality	None!	Lukewarm
Exhortation	Remember Repent	Don't fear Be faithful	Repent!	Remove Jezebel Tribulation for her followers	Wake up! Remember & repent	Hold fast!	Repent, Buy Gold, Garments Salve
Warning	I will remove Your lampstand	Prison & Testing	I will come I'll make war	Hold fast!	I will come unannounced	To the Jews	I reprove and discipline I'll spew out
Promise	Tree of life	Crown of Life	Manna & White stone	Authority with Jesus	White garments Book of Life Praised to God	Pillar in Temple Name of God "Jerusalem"	Throne

REVELATION ILLUSTRATIONS
Elders, Living Beings, the Sea of Glass

Twenty-Four Elders.

- Three possibilities.
  - 12 Patriarchs in OT: 12 Apostles: NT.
  - 24 Godly men from history.
    - OT Priests. 1 Chronicles 24:7+
    - 1st 24 in genealogy: Adam to Jacob.
  - Special class of angels.
- Arguments against angels.
  - "Elder" used for men not angels.
  - Angels don't wear crowns.
  - Angels don't need white garments.

Four Living Beings.

- Identity.

Revelation	Ezekiel
- Called living creatures.	
Revelation 4:6	Ezekiel 1:5
- Four in number.	
Revelation 4:6	Ezekiel 1:5
- Man, Lion, Ox, Eagle.	
Revelation 4:7	Ezekiel 1:120
- Near throne.	
Revelation 4:6	Ezekiel 1:22,26
- Multiple eyes.	
Revelation 4:8	Ezekiel 1:18

[Likely not a Cherubim, who were attendants of God, Ezekiel 10:20. Satan was a Cherubim, Ezekiel 28:14,16]

- Responsibilities.
  - Guard the things of God. Genesis 3:24 The Garden
  - Signify the presence of God. Exodus 25:20 The Ark

The Sea of Glass. The Peace of Heaven

- Sea of the Tabernacle (Laver). Exodus 30:18-21
- Sea in Soloman's Temple. 1 Kings 7:23-37
  Also the blood of Christ for washing away sin.

Note: Chapter 4 on pages 55-56 of the Study Guide.

REVELATION ILLUSTRATIONS
Views Concerning the Rider on the White Horse

Who Is the Rider?

- Jesus Christ.
  - Futurists. Kuyper, Ladd, Morris
  - Spiritual.
    - All scholars prior to AD 1500.
    - Most spiritual interpreters today.
- Antichrist.
  - Most Futurists. Walvoord, Ryrie, Lindsey.
  - A few spiritual interpreters who are doubters.

Reasons in support of the rider as Jesus.

- Context. Jesus is prominent in Chapters 1-5.

- White is *always* associated with holy and heavenly.
- "Conquer" or "overcome" is associated with Jesus.
  - Revelation 3:21, 5:5.
  - John 16:33.
- The rider has a crown. See Revelation14:14
- Parallel passage. Revelation 19:11
- *The Conquering Christ* is a thread through Revelation.
- Christ's mission. See Matthew 10:34.

Arguments in support of religious persecution.

- Context. Persecution follows Christ's conquest.
- Parallel passage. Matthew 10:34
- Kill. Greek: Slaughter ≠ Kill in battle.
- Revelation 6:9. Same word for Kill. Sphago
- John's message to believers being persecuted.

Note: Chapter 6 on page 61 of the Study Guide.

REVELATION ILLUSTRATIONS
Land-Based Disasters

Numerous broad categories of land-based disasters can be discerned.

- Diseases-Human.
  - In History: Bubonic Plague.
    - 6th Century. 25 million deaths in Europe.
    - 1340-1400. One third of the population of Europe died.
    - 1855-1899. China, India, Hawaii, 12.5+ million died.
  - Today: Leading Causes of Death Worldwide (Deaths per Year).
    - 1. Heart disease, 8.9 million.
    - 2. Cancers, 7.4 million.
    - 3. Cardiovascular, 5.7 million.
    - 4. Respiratory Infections, 4.1 million.
    - 5. Birth Related, 3.1 million.
    - 6. HIV Related, 1.5 million.
- Diseases-Animal.
  - Avian Flu.
  - Swine Fever.
  - Foot and Mouth Disease.
  - Infected Ticks.
    The great concern here is spread of these diseases to humans.
- Diseases-Plants.
  - Blights. Withered leaves, branches, …
  - Rusts. Fungal diseases.
  - Rot. Diseases that decay plants.
    30-50% crop loss in less-developed countries.
- Earthquakes. Deadliest in History.
  - China, 1556. 830,000 deaths.
  - China, 1976. 655,000 deaths.
  - Syria, 1138. 230,000 deaths.
  - Indonesia, 2004. 227,000 deaths.

- Haiti, 2005. 222,000 deaths.
- Volcanic Eruptions. 618 Total in Recorded History.
  - Iceland, 1783. 10,000 deaths (25% of the population).
  - Vesuvius, 79 AD. 25,000 deaths.
  - Indonesia, 1815. 71,000 deaths.
  - Indonesia, 1883. 37,000 deaths.
  - Martinique, 1902. 30,000 deaths.
- Tornadoes. Deadliest in US History.
  - Missouri, Illinois, Indiana, 1925. 695 deaths.
  - Natchez Tornado, 1840. 317 deaths.
  - St. Louis Tornado, 1896. 255 deaths.
  - Tupelo Tornado, 1936. 216 deaths.
  - Gainesville Tornado, 1936. 203 deaths.

Note: Land-Based Disasters: First Trumpet on page 71 and First Bowl on page 107 of the Study Guide.

REVELATION ILLUSTRATIONS
Maritime Disasters

Three broad categories of maritime disasters can be discerned.

- Shipwrecks in History.
  - Kianga, Philippines, 1987. 4386 deaths.
  - Dona Paz, Shanghai, 1948. 3500 deaths.
  - Joola, Gambia, 2002. 1863 deaths.
  - Sultana, US-TN, 1865. 1547 deaths.
  - Titanic, North Atlantic, 1912. 1517 deaths.
- Typhoons in History.
  - Haiphong, Vietnam, 1881. 300,000 deaths.
  - Nina, China, 1975. 229,000 deaths.
  - 1780 Typhoon, Philippines, 1780. 100,000 deaths.
  - Swatow, Philippines, 1922. 60,000 deaths.
  - China, China, 1912. 50,000 deaths.
- Tsunamis in History.
  - Indonesia, 2004. 230,000 deaths.
  - Japan, 2011. 18,000 deaths.
  - Portugal, 1755. 60,000 deaths.
  - Indonesia, 1883. 2,000 deaths.
  - Japan, 1498. 31,000 deaths.

Note: Land-Based Disasters: Second Trumpet on page 72 and Second Bowl on page 107 of the Study Guide.

REVELATION ILLUSTRATIONS
Fresh Water Disasters

At least two broad categories of fresh water disasters can be discerned.

- Floods.
  - China, 1931. 3,000,000 deaths.
  - China, 1887. 1,500,000 deaths.
  - China, 1938. 750,000 deaths.
  - China, 1975. 231,000 deaths.
  - China, 1935. 145,000 deaths.
- Droughts.
  - China, 1960. 30,000,000 deaths.
  - China, 1907. 24,000,000 deaths.
  - India, 1900. 19,000,000 deaths.
  - India, 1770. 15,000,000 deaths.
  - China, 1887. 13,000,000 deaths.

Note: Land-Based Disasters: Third Trumpet on page 72 and Third Bowl on page 107 of the Study Guide.

REVELATION ILLUSTRATIONS
Cosmic Disturbances

A few cosmic disturbances are known and suspected.

- Asteroid Collisions.
    - Yucatan Peninsula, 65 million years ago. 186 miles in diameter.
    Resulted in the extinction of 1/2 to 2/3 of all species on the planet.
    - Chesapeake Bay, 35 million years ago. 125 miles in diameter.
- Ozone Layer Depletion. Disputed cause: natural vs. manmade?
- Sunspots. Not much is known about how they affect the earth.

Note: The Sixth Seal on page 63, the Fourth Trumpet on page 72, and the Fourth Bowl on page 107 of the Study Guide.

REVELATION ILLUSTRATIONS
The Abyss, Hades, Paradise, The Lake of Fire

The Abyss (The Bottomless Pit). The abode of imprisoned demons. Luke 8:26+

Hades (Sheol, the Pit). The abode of unrepentant humans. Luke 16:19+ (Lazarus)

Paradise (Abraham's Bosom)
- The destiny of the redeemed prior to the New Jerusalem. Luke 23:43, Philippians 1:23-24.
- They are apparently visible to the residents of Hades. Luke 16:23

The Lake of Fire
- Final destiny of Satan, the Antichrist, and the False Prophet. Revelation 19:20, 20:10
- Final destiny of Death and Hell. Revelation 20:24.

Note: Chapter 9 on page 75 of the Study Guide.

REVELATION ILLUSTRATIONS
Demonic Powers

The Work of Demons: They rob the unrighteous of:
- Light, i.e., true righteousness and holiness.
- Joy and peace.
- Wisdom and understanding.

Demonic Assaults on Unbelievers
- Invasions of Rome, 500-1500 AD.
- Opium addiction in the Orient.
- Islam (600), Hinduism (1500 BC), Buddhism (500 BC), Confucianism (500 BC)
- Sexually Transmitted Diseases.
- Dark Ages, 500-1500 AD.
  - Population decline.
  - Literature, arts also.
- Renaissance, 1300-1700. Rebirth.
  - Revival of learning.
  - Man becomes the center.
- Rationalism, 1800s. Human reason is everything, no need for revelation.
- Secularism. Removal of anything religious from public discourse.
- Liberalism. Political philosophy founded on liberty and freedom.

Note: Chapter 9 on page 75 of the Study Guide.

REVELATION ILLUSTRATIONS
Wars in History

All Wars in History
- Approximately 1800 wars in recorded history.
- Usually multiple wars occurring simultaneously.
- From 100,000,000 to 1 billion killed in all wars.

Number of Wars by Historical Period
- 3100-1000 BC. 75
- 999-1 BC. 155
- 1 AD- 999 AD. 166
- 1000-1499. 172
- 1500-1799. 335
- 1800-1899. 385
- 1900-1944. 208
- 1945-1989. 176
- 1990-2002. 59
- 2003-2010. 32
- 2011-Present. 18

Note: The Fourth Seal on page 62 and the Sixth Trumpet on page 77 of the Study Guide.

REVELATION ILLUSTRATIONS
Waldenses and Albigensians

According to the Historicist Approach of interpreting Revelation the two witnesses of Chapter 11 represent the Waldenses and Albigensians, and others who resisted the Catholic Church before the Reformation.

Wandenses
- A Christian movement:
    - Started in Lyon, France. 1170
    - By Peter Waldo, a wealthy merchant.
- Advocated poverty as the way to perfection.
- Group was forerunner of the Reformation.

Albigensians
- A Reform movement in Croatia and Bulgaria.
- Advocated perfection, poverty, preaching.
- Followers were called Cathars.
- Called Albigensian because many relocated to:
    - South central France.
    - The city of Albi.
- The Albigensian or Cathar Crusade:
    - Military campaign (1209-1229),
    - Conducted by Catholic Church.
    To eliminate Catharism in France.

Note: The 1260 Days (Historicist Approach), on page 82 of the Study Guide.

REVELATION ILLUSTRATIONS
Periods of Time

According to the Spiritual Approach of interpreting Revelation there are three basic Periods of Time in the book. This can be a bit disconcerting as The Church Age is referred to by four different terms.

- The Church Age. From the Ascension to Christ's Second Coming.
  - 42 Months. Revelation 11:2, 13:5
  - 1000 Years. Revelation 20:7
  - A time, times, half a time. Revelation 12:14
  - 1260 Days. Revelation 11:3, 12:6

- A Short Duration, 3½ Days. Revelation 11:7-9,11

- The Judgment Day. Revelation 11:15+, 20:11

Note: Periods of Time (Spiritual Approach), on page 83 of the Study Guide. Also Chapters 11 and 20.

REVELATION ILLUSTRATIONS
Antichristian Governments

Here are some examples of governments in history which have opposed God's people (believers).

- Egypt. Genesis and Exodus.
- Babylon. Under Nebuchadnezzar.
- Medo-Persia. See especially Daniel and Esther.
- Greece. Under Alexander the Great and his successors.
- Rome. Emperor was to be worshiped as a god.
- Islam. ~650 in the Middle East.
- China, Japan. Emperors were gods.
- England in the 1600s.
  - Puritans.
  - Pilgrims.
- France in the 1700s. Huguenots.
- Communist Countries. 1920s until the present time.
- Muslim Countries today with "Blasphemy Laws."

Note: The Antichrist of Chapter 13 on page 93 of the Study Guide.

REVELATION ILLUSTRATIONS
False Religions and Philosophies

False Religions

- Pantheism. Greeks
- Animism. Africa, America
- Buddhism. Asia
- Hinduism. India
- Shintoism. Japan
- Atheism. Worldwide
- Islam. Middle East, North Africa
- Liberation Theology. US, Central & South America
- Science. Notably the US and Europe
- Secular Humanism. Worldwide

False Philosophies

- Rationalism. Human reason is the ultimate authority.
- Existentialism. The individual is free and responsible.
- Communism. The means of production, distribution, and exchange owned by the state.
- Freudian Psychology. Bogus theories about unconscious/unconscious mental processes.
- Darwinism. Theory of biological evolution based on random mutation and natural selection.

Note: The False Prophet of Chapter 13 on page 94 of the Study Guid

10406704R00096

Made in the USA
Lexington, KY
21 September 2018